Three Saints

To

Father Pite Alliata,

Enjoy "Three Saints"

Best wishes,

Joan Williams

THREE SAINTS
Women Who Changed History

Genevieve of Paris
Catherine of Siena
Teresa of Avila

Joan Williams

THREE SAINTS
Women Who Changed History: Genevieve of Paris, Catherine of Siena, Teresa of Avila
by Joan Williams

Edited by Marcia Broucek
Cover design by Tom A. Wright
Text design and typesetting by Patricia A. Lynch

Photo credits: Erich Lessing/Art Resource, New York

Published by ACTA Publications, 5559 W. Howard Street, Skokie, IL 60077
(800) 397-2282 www.actapublications.com.

Library of Congress Number: 2006931876
ISBN 10: 0-87946-315-5
ISBN 13: 978-0-87946-315-1
Printed in the United States of America
Year: 15 14 13 12 10 9 8 7 6
Printing: 10 9 8 7 6 5 4 3 2 1

Contents

For Mari, Terese, Kathy, Barb, Lou, Sean
and in loving memory of Lisa (1965-1977)

Introduction

Traditional accounts of the lives of women saints have given scant attention to their influence in public affairs. Because biographers have focused mainly on their personal holiness and miraculous powers, stories of their bold and daring actions have too often been neglected. One exception, of course, is Joan of Arc. Much scholarly and popular interest has concentrated on St. Joan because of her exceptional, highly visible military leadership. But biographers' attention to her exploits, and their slight of those of other saintly women, has left us with the impression that their accomplishments were insignificant in comparison.

Recently, however, I chanced to open a typical book about the lives of saints; the kind of book that is really a collection of idealizing sermons extolling their virtues. St. Genevieve of Paris (c. 422-512) caught my attention. The author noted Genevieve's efforts to save the Parisians from Attila the Hun, rescue the people from starvation by leading a caravan of boats through a barbarian blockade, and repeatedly persuade Frankish chieftains to release captives—all summarized in a few sentences. Such skimpy treatment left me wondering about the rest of the story. Descriptions of the complexity of each situation, as well as Genevieve's grasp of political strategy and tactics, were missing.

Three women saints in particular have captured my attention and interest: Genevieve of Paris, Catherine of Siena, and Teresa of Avila. They were born in different countries of Western Europe and lived during widely dissimilar historical periods spanning the fifth to the sixteenth century. I did not expect to find these women engaged in courageous political action during times often considered less enlightened than our own. Each was involved in significant political actions that changed history, and their efforts to reform church and state, despite overwhelming opposition, surprised me.

While a complete description of their contributions to history is not possible in this short book, I hope to draw attention to their neglected stories, their influence, and their accomplishments.

Genevieve of Paris (c. 422-512), despite threats against her life, prevented Parisians from fleeing to certain death when they panicked over an imminent attack by Attila the Hun. Later she emboldened Parisians to stand firm against the barbarian leader Clovis while she negotiated governing terms with him.

Catherine of Siena (1347-1380) braved prejudice against women active in any sphere other than home or convent and involved herself in Italian politics of both church and state. She pressured wavering Pope Gregory XI to keep his promise to return the papacy from Avignon to Rome. In hundreds of letters to kings, queens, military leaders and civic officials, she gave advice concerning the pressing problems of her time. She sent scorching letters to cardinals admonishing them against corruption. During a period of widespread violence, she negotiated a number of peace agreements, including one between Florence and the Holy See.

Teresa of Avila (1515-1582) challenged the status quo of both Spanish society and the Church by rejecting the practice of labeling certain individuals "honorable" and looking down on others who did not have socially acceptable ancestry. She overturned the longstanding tradition of aristocratic dominance over Carmelite convents. Through political skill and personal charisma, she prevailed over those who opposed her reforms. In an age of suspicion and repression by torture, she constantly had to outwit the watchdogs of the Inquisition because she encouraged the practice of "mental prayer," which was considered dangerous at the time.

Traditionally, women saints have been esteemed by Christians as ideal role models for women. But the image most often presented has been that of holy and miraculous otherness, an image out of the reach of us mortals. My research has uncovered a more complex and varied image of these women saints, revealing bold, daring actions in public life that grew out of their private, spiritual lives.

My goal in *Three Saints* is to widen our limited view by focusing on the concrete actions and decisions these women took in their day-to-day public lives. I have included historical background and cultural details of their times to give a sense of the reality and complexity of their involvement in public life. What were the political challenges they faced? How did they overcome the cultural and religious restrictions under which they lived so they could pursue their goals? What political successes and failures did they experience?

We are often told that the saints were people "just like us." But there is nothing like the messy world of politics to show real human struggles. Conflict, confusion, controversy and criticism are all part of the human condition, as well as successes and failures. For Genevieve, Catherine and Teresa, their engagement in public affairs was an important and essential part of their holy lives.

I

St. Genevieve of Paris

Fearless Leader

"Saint Genoveva" by Hugo van der Goes (d. 1482). Grisaille. Sawed-off reverse side.
Left wing of the Fall (40-01-01-59) from the Diptych of the Fall and the Redemption.
Oil on oakwood, (c. 1470) 33.8 x 23 cm – Inv. 945,5822 A.
Photo Credit: Erich Lessing / Art Resource, NY
Kunsthistorisches Museum, Vienna, Austria

Chapter 1
GENEVIEVE'S PROMISE

In the fifth century A.D., widespread barbarian attacks hammered away at the crumbling Roman Empire. No frontier was safe. Destruction and pillage followed the barbarian invaders, who provoked fear and panic among inhabitants everywhere. Even rumors of barbarian threats paralyzed citizens and weakened their defenses.

During these turbulent times, the Franks—one of the most organized of barbarian tribes—invaded Gaul, an area that included the future country of France. In piecemeal fashion they gradually conquered territory still under the authority of the Western Roman Empire. The city of Lutece, which later became Paris, grew increasingly vulnerable because of its strategic central location. Frankish chieftains looked at Paris as a military prize to be won at all costs.

A few miles from Paris, in the small village of Nanterre, Genevieve was born around the year 422. She was the only child of Severus and Gerontia—a child for whom they had yearned and prayed. This future patron saint of Paris spent her formative years in the midst of the political turmoil swirling about her. Joël Schmidt, a historian of Roman antiquity, tells us that both sides of Genevieve's family were involved militarily and civically in society.

Genevieve's father, Severus, had spent his youth in military camps defending Roman lands in Gaul against invaders, and he later served as an elite officer commanding the Federate Franks. The Federates were a group of barbarian Franks who had become allies of Rome and joined the Gallo-Roman army. Because of his military experience and natural gift of leadership, Severus was chosen to become governor of the lands of the Roman Empire in the area of Gaul called Lyonnaise the Fourth, which included Paris.[1] Genevieve's grandfather had also been a military man, a general in the Gallo-Roman army, and a personal friend of Constantine III, the Roman Emperor of the West.[2] It is not hard to imagine that young Genevieve heard visiting generals and dignitaries discussing military strategies for the many crises facing Gaul.[3]

Severus and his wife, Gerontia, practiced Catholic Christianity and were respected by the townspeople for their leadership, religious piety, and generosity in the active Christian community in Nanterre. As the Western Roman Empire continued to disintegrate, the Church filled the vacuum by establishing order, providing food, and looking after the security of inhabitants. Severus was particularly helpful in rebuilding the agriculture economy of Nanterre, which had been destroyed during the barbarian invasions. In addition to their civic commitment, Genevieve's parents gave much of their personal wealth to charities for the needy.

As leaders in the community, they saw to it that Genevieve received the education reserved to members of the Gallo-Roman aristocracy, and Severus took her on many of his trips throughout the area, exposing her to the politics of the region.[4] As her education progressed, they also noticed that Genevieve, from an early age, demonstrated an unusual tendency toward prayer, holy conduct, and eager participation in religious services.

A Fateful Meeting

In 429, when Genevieve was seven years old, she met Bishops Germanus of Auxerre and Lupus of Troyes. The bishops had stopped to visit the parish in Nanterre on their way to Britain, where at the order of Pope Celestine I they would fight the spread of Pelagianism, a heresy that rejected the doctrine of original sin.

Because he was a leading dignitary in Nanterre, Severus and his wife and daughter led the crowd of people greeting the bishops. Bishop Germanus is said to have immediately recognized the gifted spiritual nature of young Genevieve. It proved to be a fortuitous meeting. Church leaders were on the lookout for charismatic individuals who could be inspiring examples of holiness to people during this time of religious and political upheaval.

Germanus approached Genevieve and asked her if she would consecrate herself to Christ. According to the ancient Latin life of Genevieve, *Vita Sanctae Genovefae,* she responded, "Blessings on you, my Father, for your suggestion, which is perhaps your own wish, is indeed the very thing I long for. It is my wish, Holy Father, and I pray that the Lord will deign to answer my prayer."

Germanus replied, "Have faith, my daughter, and act manfully. What you believe in your heart and declare with your mouth, you must strive to fulfill in your deeds. For the Lord will give you strength and fortitude for your adornment."[5]

The next day Bishop Germanus asked Genevieve if she remembered the promise she had made to consecrate herself to Christ. She replied, "I remember, Holy Father, what I promised to God and to you."[6] Germanus then gave her a copper coin with a cross carved on it as a religious talisman to remind her of her promise. He instructed her to have the coin pierced so she could hang it on a chain to wear around her neck.

Perhaps one of the most startling details of this exchange

is the bishop's use of the word "manfully" (the Latin text of the *Vita* reads "*viriliter*"). Here we are in the fifth century, and a bishop of the Roman Catholic Church is advising a young girl to act like a man. It is telling that Genevieve's biographer, whom historians believe to have been a priest from Burgundy, neither censored nor questioned the use of "manfully." Apparently it was a quality considered both acceptable and desirable in young Genevieve.

A few days later, Genevieve's strength and determination were put to the test. Her mother, Gerontia, was preparing to go to church for a solemn feast day and ordered Genevieve to stay at home. Genevieve, wanting to go along, sobbed and pleaded: "With Christ's support, I will keep the vow I made to Saint Germanus."[7]

Angered by what she thought was Genevieve's disobedience, her mother boxed her ears, and the *Vita* reports that Gerontia was struck blind for two years. Eventually, Gerontia came to understand that her daughter was trying to fulfill the promise she had made to Bishop Germanus. One day she asked Genevieve to bring her water from a nearby well and, after dabbing water on her eyes, Gerontia was cured of her blindness.[8]

Taking the Veil

Around fifteen years of age, Genevieve formalized the religious commitment she had made to Bishop Germanus as a child and took the veil of a dedicated virgin. As the required age for consecration at that time was twenty-five, Genevieve needed and received a dispensation from the diocese of Lutece. No doubt Bishop Germanus, who had become her spiritual mentor, approved that dispensation. We are told that she was clothed for the ceremony in a white tunic and a mauve veil, which was held in place by the medal the bishop had given her.

After her formal dedication to Christ, Genevieve joined the community of women in Nanterre devoted to prayer and charity. As there were no nunneries in Paris in the fifth century, Genevieve continued to live with her parents. By this time, the military discussions she had heard as a child had moved into debates about the growing power of a general named Attila and his ferocious horsemen, the Huns.

In 437, Genevieve's father met with Roman General Aetius, the successor to Genevieve's grandfather, and learned that Attila's Huns had helped Aetius win a battle against the Burgundian barbarians. While this was initially good news, the Huns' crucial role in the battle gave them a heightened sense of power. Concerned, Severus warned of future trouble and predicted that the Huns would eventually break their fragile allegiance to the Empire, putting Gaul at their mercy.[9] Years later Genevieve would see her father's prediction come true and remember the insight her father had given her into Attila's character, motives and goals.

During the very cold winter of 439-440, when Genevieve was seventeen, Severus became ill and died. Genevieve's mother, despondent over the death of her husband, died a few days later. Genevieve had the warm support of her community of women friends to help her survive this severe blow.

Because the Council of Hipone of 393 A.D. stipulated that after the death of parents virgins had to be given to the care of mature, wise women of piety, Genevieve moved to Paris to live with her godmother aunt. A devout woman and a successful businesswoman, she welcomed Genevieve to her home and provided valuable assistance in administering the considerable wealth Genevieve had inherited from her parents.

During this period of the Middle Ages, women's rights to inherit gave them freedom and power to act outside the home. Genevieve had vast farmlands of wheat fields in the areas of Meaux and Melun—towns located short distances from Paris—which she skillfully managed from the growing to the marketing stages. She took many trips to her farmlands, becoming familiar with the local areas and making friends with the people—contacts that would become crucial later on.

Although her productive farms made a comfortable life possible, Genevieve continued to live in austerity, devoting herself to helping the poor and distributing her wealth to charities.

Inheriting a Political Role

The Roman Code of Theodosius, under which Romanized Franks lived, stipulated that military officials returning to civilian life automatically be given a high municipal function. The code further stated that when the daughter of such a person was the only descendant, she was to be given the same function. This meant that Genevieve inherited her father's position as a high ranking municipal official. She carried out this role as one of the top magistrates of the city council of Paris, which gave her access to civic and political information that was not available to the general population.[10]

It also plunged her into the middle of the city's increasing refugee problem. Refugees fleeing the encroachment of the barbarians in the countryside were crowding the center of Paris. The *Ile de la Cité*, or "Island of the City," provided some protection from attack because it was surrounded by the River Seine. Genevieve devoted herself to ministering to sick and injured refugees, and her strong faith and encouragement raised the spirits and hopes of these frightened people. In his book *Sainte Genevieve*, Schmidt suggests that she also carried a purse of Roman gold coins that she generously distributed to the needy.[11]

As Genevieve cared for wounded soldiers at the military camps on the left bank of the Seine, she stayed in touch with military events. Along with other dedicated women, she listened to stories of devastation told by soldiers returning from the battlefield and refugees fleeing hostilities. While she showed compassion toward those who were suffering, she also expressed confidence in the survival of their world.

Genevieve was a realist who did not live in a cloud of bliss and theological dreams. She understood the political nuances of the world she lived in, and she responded bravely to difficulties and threatening events.[12] When word finally came that Attila and his Huns had charged into Gaul, Genevieve was ready to face her first big test of courage.

Chapter 2
ATTILA'S THREAT

In 451 the citizens of Paris got word that Attila and his Huns were attacking the province of Gaul. Attila had earned a reputation for being "the most hated man in the world"—a reputation he made every effort to enhance. He ruthlessly sacked cities and towns for their resources, even murdering his own brother to gain power. When rumor inflated the number of Attila's victims from ten to a thousand, he considered the fear it caused helpful to his goals.[1]

The refugees who had fled to Paris brought with them not only wounds but nightmares from the forefront of the advancing Huns. To them the Huns were "wild beasts walking upright."[2] But Attila was not "barbarian" in the sense we think of today; he was not a stupid brute. In fact, just the opposite was true. Attila knew how the Roman Empire worked, and he was a cunning strategist. These qualities, combined with his tenacity and refusal to be intimidated, made him a formidable foe.

Fearful that Attila would soon rampage Paris, the Parisians panicked and prepared to flee. They gathered in front of the city government office and demanded that the city council evacuate the city. Genevieve, a council magistrate, remained calm and told the people that God would save them if they prayed.

Genevieve had sound, practical reasons for opposing the evacuation. First, she knew the lay of the land. Impenetrable forests in which wild boars and bears roamed surrounded Paris, leaving people nowhere to flee. Second, she based her decision on clear, logical analysis of the political and military information she had received.[3] Since Attila's army was coming from the northeast, and the Gallo-Roman army and Visigoths from the south, all possible roads out of the city would be a trap for fleeing Parisians. Furthermore, she knew that if the inhabitants escaped toward the west there were no resources available and they would end up cornered at the ocean.

It is reasonable to assume that Genevieve hoped praying would calm the citizens' panic, freeing them to listen to reason and to reconsider their dangerous escape plan. However, like many politicians who take an unpopular stand, Genevieve received insults and threats and had to be protected by soldiers. But she continued to argue her position, urging the inhabitants to trust her.

But no one listened. It is conceivable that many were suspicious of her Frank origin, believing she may have had a secret pact with Attila to give up the city without a fight.[4] The men, especially, ignored her protests. Genevieve went so far as to follow them to the bridge that led to the mainland, trying to persuade them to stay. But when some angry citizens tried to stone her, Genevieve finally took refuge in the baptistry of the small church of St. Jean-en-Rond on the top of a hill.

Against the wishes of their husbands, many wives of city leaders followed her and locked themselves inside the church. In the end, their prayers and protest proved successful: The men would not leave the city without the women.[5]

While the women were praying in the church, Genevieve received word that Attila was on the road between Reims and Troyes, heading toward Orleans. Genevieve's analysis—which concurred with military opinion—was that there was no tactical advantage for Attila to come to Paris. It would be more to his advantage to go directly to Orleans, where he could presumably take the city quickly because of his previous alliance with the king who controlled the city. Genevieve's analysis proved correct, but Attila and his Huns were in Orleans only one day when the armies of Aetius and Theodoric arrived to chase him out.[6]

Death Threats

The Parisians panicked again when they heard that Attila was retreating and heading in their direction. Thinking that Attila would surely take Paris as revenge or sack it for much-needed resources for his army, the Parisian men once again prepared to flee. But Genevieve and the women who had joined her in the church held their ground. They believed the people of Paris could sustain a siege.[7] When Genevieve came out of the church to try to talk to the men, they called her a false prophetess who was trying to prevent them from moving to safety and conspired to kill her by stoning or drowning.

According to the *Vita* of Genevieve, the fortunate appearance of Archdeacon Sedulius from Auxerre saved Genevieve's life. Sedulius had witnessed the revered Bishop Germanus giving magnificent testimony for Genevieve, and he championed her cause. Addressing the crowd assembled to plan her death, Sedulius pleaded, "Oh citizens, don't consent to such a crime! For we have heard our Primate Germanus say that this woman, whose murder you are plotting, was chosen by God from her mother's womb. And behold, I present these eulogies direct from Saint Germanus."[8]

The word of the Archdeacon and these "eulogies"—objects that were blessed by the bishop—saved the day for Genevieve. Persuaded that she was a most faithful servant of God, and filled with the fear of God, the citizens gave up their plan to attack her.

Meanwhile, it is not likely that Attila even thought of attacking Paris because it would have been out of his way. Attila and his mounted Huns traveled at a runaway pace trying to escape the armies of Aetius and Theodoric, but the Gallo-Roman army caught up with them about sixty miles from Paris, at a place called the Catalaunian Plains.

The inhabitants of Paris anxiously awaited news from the battlefront, which was to be communicated through a relay of torches. If the torches were extinguished, it would mean that Attila had won. If Aetius won, a second torch was to be lit. Confident that Attila would not come to Paris, Genevieve predicted his defeat.

When she saw the second torch was lit, Genevieve knew she had foreseen the outcome accurately: "After a gory and demoralizing bout of close-quarter combat," Attila retreated and withdrew from Gaul.[9]

Overnight Heroine

News of the victory made Genevieve an overnight heroine. The people credited her prayers for preventing the Hun army from surrounding and attacking Paris, and they carried her through the city in triumph.[10] Her new heroine status contrasted sharply with the earlier death threats she had received. Her equanimity in the face of both public reactions demonstrated not only her strong faith but also her understanding of the ups and downs of fame and misfortune.

A period of stability followed the defeat of Attila, and Paris experienced a time of peace and reconstruction. Genevieve contributed much of her wealth to develop commerce, and she encouraged artisans to return and repopulate the city.[11] Her reputation for holiness continued to grow, along with popular esteem for her courage during the threatened siege of Paris.

During this time, Genevieve is reported to have performed many miracles, including healing individuals afflicted with blindness, paralysis, and other illnesses. The *Vita* tells the story of Genevieve's miraculous ability to rekindle an extinguished candle: "A candle which no spark had touched, kindled itself, by divine consent, at the touch of her hand." Many invalids "who procured a fragment of that candle were soon restored to pristine health."[12] To this day, the traditional icon of Genevieve depicts her holding a candle that the devil is trying to extinguish.

Miracles were a powerful force in the early Middle Ages, since all forms of disease were considered to be supernatural in origin.[13] People looked to religious people for cures rather than to doctors. If a person could perform miracles, it was proof of a right relation with the supernatural and true "mystic potency," whereas false "mystic potency" was associated with demons and evil deeds.[14] Historian Ernest Brehaut helps put this in context: "Many miracles were real: for example, the cessation of a pain or a natural recovery from a sickness would be regarded as a miracle."[15] Genevieve's holiness, her deep faith, and her compassion had a therapeutic effect on people's fear and anxiety during those troubled times, which contributed to the miracle of their healing.

A New Threat

The period of political stability following the defeat of Attila did not last. After Pope Leon I died in 461, his successor, Pope Hilarus, was more concerned with fighting the spread of the Arian heresy than with saving the Empire. His neglect is thought by some to have speeded up the end of the Western Roman Empire.

Genevieve realized that the Empire would soon fall, and she knew that the Franks under the leadership of Childeric had the discipline and power to take over and control northern Gaul. Being a political pragmatist, she took on the role of intermediary between the Parisians and the Franks. Her friendship with Childeric, the Franks' king, as well as with

Aegidius, the Roman army general, made negotiation between the two sides possible.[16]

When the Roman Empire ultimately abandoned the lands north of the Loire River, Childeric was in position to take over and the Franks became the military "protectors" of the Parisians. But as more and more Franks moved to Paris, Paris soon found its Roman population outnumbered by the Frankish people, and the upheaval and instability of the city persisted.

Genevieve continued to manage her vast agricultural enterprise north of Paris and in Meaux, where she still had the fields inherited from her parents and from her aunt. As the Bishop Germanus had predicted, Genevieve provided a living example of holiness and moral courage, continuing to work miracles and breaking through the depression of many sick people and giving them reason to live.[17]

It is not surprising that Genevieve became the *de facto* leader of the Christian community. One interesting note highlights Genevieve's power at the time. Schmidt observes that history has not retained the names of priests that succeeded the bishop position in Paris from 451 to the death of Genevieve over sixty years later. It was as if her personality and leadership eclipsed formal Church authority during that time.[18]

Chapter 3
GENEVIEVE'S TRIUMPH

The situation for Paris—and Genevieve—changed dramatically in 481 when Childeric died and his son Clovis was crowned king of the Franks. From his youth, Clovis had a passion for war and a willingness to face death if defeated, and now he wanted to take control not only of Paris but also of the rest of Gaul. He decided to attack Syagrius, the last Roman ruler in Gaul. When the Franks won the battle, Clovis had Syagrius beheaded in front of his troops in a move calculated to demonstrate his power. This barbarian action appalled Genevieve and made her fear for the Christian community in Gaul.[1]

Clovis' victory greatly expanded the territory he wanted to establish as his kingdom, but he faced resistance from the inhabitants of the conquered region. Clovis lost no time in establishing a blockade around Paris to force the opposition to surrender. To add to the misery, the Franks prevented people from traveling to areas outside the city to get food, which resulted in widespread hunger and starvation. As the siege stretched out, fear spread among the people, demoralizing and weakening them.

Legend tells us that Genevieve led the resistance of the Parisians. She was not intimidated by Clovis' tactics and refused to stand by and watch the people of Paris give in because they were starving. Standing up to his brute force, Genevieve warned Clovis that he would never be accepted as a ruler of the city unless he and his warriors converted to Catholic Christianity. Her insistence added to that of Clovis' Christian wife, Clotilde, who had repeatedly urged Clovis to convert to the one true God. But Clovis was not interested; he and his warriors wanted to remain faithful to their pagan gods.

Although Clovis knew he could take Paris by force, he did not want to destroy the antique Roman monuments remaining in Paris. He dreamed of recreating the great classical civilization that had built those treasures. By systematically demoralizing and weakening the citizens, he hoped the people of Paris would give up willingly.[2] The siege is said to have been prolonged for about ten years, with varying degrees of intimidation by the Franks causing widespread suffering.

A Secret Plan

The turning point came in 493 when Clovis' first-born son died. Clovis lashed out in anger by reinforcing the blockade of Paris. Many Parisians died of hunger, and others felt discouraged and defeated. Genevieve reacted to this new threat by initiating a secret plan to get food for the starving Parisians.

As a city council member, Genevieve had authority to use the imperial transport services for official purposes, and she made plans to travel to her farms outside of Paris to get grain. She carefully considered three options to bypass the blockade. The first possibility was to go down the River Seine, but its winding flow and slow current would take too long, risking the chance of exposing her and the boaters to the Franks. Even if they traveled in the dark of night, the long trip could last well into daylight. The second option was to go against the current of the Seine. But rowing against the current, with the noise of the agitated water, might alert the Frank guards and expose the party to danger. The third option was to travel by road, but the roads were dangerous because of highway robbers, barbarians, and an ongoing civil war.[3]

In the end, Genevieve chose the second route. She equipped a fleet of eleven boats in secret and camouflaged them. On one moonless night in 495, Genevieve and the hired oarsmen started on their perilous journey to Arcis. As they navigated the river, they had to be constantly on alert for Franks patrolling the banks of the river. After ten hours they reached Melun, a town southeast of Paris. Genevieve and the oarsmen reasoned that Melun, located beyond the area patrolled by the Franks, would provide a safe place for a much-needed brief stop.

When they resumed their journey, shortly before dawn, they found themselves up against a dam installed by the Franks. The *Vita* describes the oarsmen as frightened and tormented by blasts of the dam's putrid odor, which they imagined to have come from "varicolored monsters."[4] Historian Joël Schmidt suggests that the Franks had set up a blockade by attaching tree trunks to a poplar that had fallen across the water. Cadavers of animals had been trapped by the dam, and the foul odor accumulated.[5]

Genevieve ordered the oarsmen to use their swords to cut the ropes that held the trees together. This broke up the dam and freed the cadavers to flow downriver, and the convoy was able to continue on its journey. They reached the town of Arcis a week after their departure from Paris.

While in Arcis, Genevieve negotiated with city officials and local priests to provide storage barns for the grain harvest produced by her fields. Planning ahead, she also secured an agreement to use the port of Arcis for future trips to get boatloads of grain.[6]

Realizing that there would not be enough grain in her harvest to feed the population of Paris, Genevieve then went to Troyes, four miles south of Arcis, to get more grain. She was well-known and revered in Troyes because of the many miracles she had worked there, and the authorities and many inhabitants were willing to help her. They put together carts filled with food and grain, which Genevieve offered to pay for, but many refused her money, making their gift an offering to God.[7]

At last the fleet of boats loaded with grain were ready to head toward Paris. But they were not out of danger yet. According to the ancient *Vita*, the flotilla was buffeted by a storm and at risk of sinking because the boats were heavy with grain. It is reported that "quickly Genevieve, her hands stretched toward heaven, begged Christ for assistance. Immediately, the ships were righted and thus through her our God and Lord saved eleven grain-laden ships." The oarsmen traveling with her were greatly relieved, and they praised God by singing the canticles of the Exodus, thanking God for saving them through the prayers of his servant Genevieve.[8]

Finally, the boats returned safely to Paris.

We may never know whether Genevieve and her companions survived this difficult trip without the Franks' knowledge. It is quite possible that Clovis and his officers knew about it but closed their eyes so as to not alienate Genevieve and the population of Paris. Holy people were held in high esteem, and Clovis knew that Genevieve was revered by the Parisians. Since he was scheming to take Paris, he did not want any further resistance by the inhabitants.[9] As historian Edward James points out, "Even pagans can recognize the importance of placating those with spiritual power."[10]

Regardless of whether the Franks were aware of what Genevieve and her brave companions were up to, it took considerable faith, courage and self-confidence on her part to risk the dangerous trip. Genevieve willingly braved the danger, relying on her faith and the weight of her spiritual reputation, to help the people of Paris.

But arriving with the grain was not the end of the problem. Faced with desperate crowds of hungry people, Genevieve stepped in once again to provide leadership. To prevent anarchy, she instructed town authorities and helpers to establish order along the wharf, stack the grain, and protect it from rain. Announcers were sent to each street of the city with instructions for assembling the population. With assistance from her female companions, Genevieve distributed the grain, giving priority to the poor and to those who were especially weakened from hunger.[11]

Genevieve's acts of courage and mercy restored the spirit and determination of the Parisians to hold out against Clovis. The Franks, in turn, faced with this renewed resistance, lightened their siege on Paris. But they continued to hold fast to their goal of one day ruling the city.

New Demands

When Clovis realized the Parisians were not ready to give up, he tried another approach, that of diplomacy. Perhaps he was simply playing for time while deciding what to do next, or perhaps he was waiting for other tactics to take effect. Whatever his motives, he decided to send ambassadors to try to persuade Genevieve to give up Paris. If she agreed to his demands, he knew the citizens would follow.

Genevieve skillfully responded, repeatedly sending the ambassadors back with the same answer each time: Clovis would have to convert to Christianity before Paris would open its gates.[12] Her unwillingness to cave in to the diplomatic pressure of Clovis raised the spirit of the population and gave people courage to continue their resistance.

Meanwhile, Clovis was forced to send his army in another direction, to fight the Alamans in the regions of Verdun and Nantes. Genevieve took advantage of his preoccupation to plan a permanent route for convoys to make repeated trips to Arcis for grain. She knew that the grain gathered on her first trip was not enough to continue to feed the hungry Parisians, so she mapped out a route for the boaters to procure grain on a regular basis, advising them to travel in small groups under the cover of night to avoid being seen.[13]

Chroniclers tell us that in 496, Clovis and his army were

losing their battle against the Alamans. On the verge of being defeated, Clovis remembered that his Christian wife, Clotilde, had frequently urged him to embrace Christianity. In desperation, Clovis promised Jesus Christ that he would be baptized if he won the battle.[14] Once he did, Clovis began to see the benefit of Christianity and decided to keep his promise to be baptized. When the news of his conversion, along with a number of his officers reached Paris, a joyful Genevieve is said to have opened the gates of the city to Clovis.[15]

Shortly afterward, Clovis established his residence in Paris, making it the center of French political power. Clovis set himself up as "defender of both Roman tradition and the Christian faith" and became the protector of bishops. Yet Clovis was not satisfied. He still dreamed of controlling all of Gaul and continued to fight battles to expand his kingdom.[16]

Clovis' conversion to Christianity appears to have been skin-deep, at best. His actions certainly did not match his professed beliefs. He displayed cruelty toward rivals and relatives. He killed off all the leading members of his family to prevent any one of them from becoming a threat to his power. Not even a distant cousin would dare claim kinship.[17] He was equally harsh toward prisoners taken in battle. After a campaign against the Visigoths, Clovis returned to Paris with a large number of prisoners whom he planned to execute.

When Genevieve learned of Clovis' intentions, she implored him to release the prisoners. Surprisingly, he did. The *Vita* says that Clovis repeatedly pardoned and released prisoners "for love of the holy virgin."[18] A political opportunist, Clovis most likely granted Genevieve's request because he recognized the benefits he could gain from performing Christian acts.

In return, he asked for Genevieve's promise to intercede with municipal magistrates and Church authorities to build a basilica in honor of Saints Peter and Paul. Since Paris was the capital of the kingdom of the Franks, Clovis thought a basilica would enhance the city's prestige, as well as his own.[19] And if he were the architect of the basilica, he thought he could strengthen his influence over Paris.

Secretly, however, Clovis wanted to build the church so he and his wife could be buried there—along with Genevieve. It was considered a privilege reserved for few to be buried close to the grave of a saint.[20] People were drawn to saints' tombs for protection and healing "because the saint in Heaven was believed to be 'present' at his tomb on earth."[21]

Genevieve, too, understood the religious and political significance of building the basilica, and she gave her support to what she considered a temple built for the glory of God. She saw the erection of a church named after Saints Peter and Paul as a demonstration of the alliance between Christianity and the Franks, and a visual reminder of Clovis' intention not to destroy Roman influence.[22]

Shortly after the basilica was completed, Genevieve died on January 3 in 512, after nearly ninety years of sainted life. She was buried at the basilica and many miracles were subsequently reported at her tomb. Over the centuries, many miracles and charitable works have been attributed to the holiness of her life. Perhaps the most famous miracle is said to have occurred in 1129 during a deadly epidemic in Paris that killed countless citizens. The Parisians invoked Genevieve's intercession, and the epidemic came to an end. Later, the church was renamed for her.

As a young girl, Genevieve had dedicated herself to Christ, and she kept her promise throughout her long life. She influenced her world not only by her exemplary holiness but also through her natural political talent, organizational ability, and clear-thinking skills. The scope and variety of civic and political actions she engaged in for a woman living in the fifth century is astounding. Genevieve clearly transcended the stereotype of women saints as passive and submissive and having no influence in public life. An exceptional woman and the patron saint of Paris, Genevieve is an inspiring heroine whose life speaks to modern women and men fifteen centuries after her death.

II

ST. CATHERINE OF SIENA

Diplomat

"Saint Catherine of Siena" by Andrea Vanni (c.1332-c.1414).
Photo Credit: Scala / Art Resource, NY
S. Domenico, Siena, Italy

Chapter 4
FROM PRAYER CELL
TO POLITICAL HELL

On June 22, 1378, thirty-one-year-old Catherine Benincasa stood on a terraced hillside near the Ponte Vecchio in Florence, Italy, and waited as an angry crowd stormed up the hill. Flames from burning buildings lit the darkness, and Catherine could see the bloody rioting in the town below. She could hear the threatening sounds of brandishing swords and knives as the crowd shouted, "Where is Catherine?" and threatened to "burn her alive or cut her into pieces."[1]

The Catholic Church and antipapist Italians had been battling fiercely, and Pope Gregory XI had sent Catherine to Florence to settle a feud between the papacy and Florence. However, before she could achieve that goal, civil war had broken out and Catherine had been caught in the middle.

Violence was a daily occurrence in the city-states of fourteenth-century Italy. Rivalries between cities existed side by side with rivalries between leading families within the cities. Long-standing feuds between pro-pope and pro-emperor factions continued to fester long after the labels lost meaning. Power changed hands so frequently that the poet Dante wrote, "The laws which the Sienese make in October are not valid in November."[2] In one instance, a ruling family in Siena lasted only three weeks before being overthrown.

Florentine leaders who were opposed to a settlement with the papacy used the outbreak of violence as an opportunity to attack Catherine.

"Where is the damned woman? Where is Catherine?" the crowd shouted.

Concerned for the safety of a small group of friends accompanying her, Catherine told them to stay in the garden behind her friend's house on the hill. Catherine bravely went to meet the angry crowd.

Boldly, she answered, "I am Catherine. Do what God allows you to do, but do not touch my companions."[3]

The leader of the mob was so startled by her response that he and his followers ran away. Perhaps the rioters, living in an age of widespread superstition, were threatened by a power they had not met before.

Later when Catherine wrote to her friend and confessor Raymond of Capua about the event, she expressed disappointment that they had denied her this opportunity for martyrdom. But she changed her mind when she realized that her death would have been used as an excuse for increased violence between the warring parties.[4]

Catherine had come a long way from her prayer cell at home to the center of never-ending political battles. She was born on April 19, 1347 in the tiny Tuscan hill town of Siena, twenty-one miles south of Florence. Dominated by palaces and towers built of warm-toned Siena brick, the medieval town was surrounded by rich farmland of olive groves and orchards. Fountains were located in every one of the city's seventeen neighborhoods, and Catherine frequently walked down the stone-paved road to the well of Fonte Branda to draw water for her family. Later in her many letters, she repeatedly drew on this imagery of fountains and water.

Catherine was the twenty-fourth of twenty-five children of Giacomo di Benincasa and his wife, Lapa di Puccio di Piacenti. According to Catherine's biographer, Raymond of Capua, her parents were virtuous, God-fearing people. Catherine is said to have received her determination and incredible physical strength from her mother. After bearing twenty-five children, Lapa lived past the age of eighty—a remarkable feat in a period when life expectancy for women was thirty years and many died in childbirth.

From her father, Catherine inherited a predisposition to patience and endurance. In the face of unjust accusations that threatened the loss of all his property, he remained even-tempered, confident that the truth would triumph.[5] Giacomo's skill as a wool dyer was much in demand in Siena. He rented a three-story home from the wool dyers guild, which housed his large family as well as a dye shop where he mixed and manufactured colors for dyeing woolen cloth.

Paintings of Catherine show her to have had the large, dark eyes and light skin features of many Tuscans. As a young child, she was sociable, lively and charming, but had her own need for solitude. She could cheer people who were despondent and was exceptionally prudent in conversation. Catherine shared the Tuscan love of flowers and often arranged miniature bouquets to give to her friends.

At age six, everything changed for Catherine. Walking home from visiting her married sister, who lived near the city gate of Porta Sant'Ansano, Catherine saw a vision across a distant valley. Above the church of the Friars Preachers, she saw the Lord Jesus Christ dressed in papal attire, seated on a royal throne surrounded by St. Peter and St. Paul. Catherine later told her biographer that when the Savior smiled on her and gave her his blessing, she felt rooted in the public roadway. Her brother Stefano, who had accompanied her, pulled her out of her trance, and she tearfully followed him home.

The experience had a powerful effect on Catherine. She

became more silent and reserved, giving her attention over to daily prayer and meditation, as well as to the practice of an extreme form of asceticism, fasting for hours and scourging her body. By age seven, Catherine had made a solemn vow of virginity and dedicated herself to Christ.

While these devotional behaviors may seem extreme today, historian Richard Kieckhefer reminds us that we need to view this devotional behavior in context.[6] The spiritual viewpoint of fourteenth-century Christians was shaped by harsh living conditions, such as famine, plagues and political upheavals that were a constant threat to their lives. The idea that these maladies were a punishment for sin contributed to the "penitential fervor of the era."[7] Through practices such as penance, fasting, abstinence, chastity and sleep deprivation, people hoped to earn for themselves a better life in heaven.

When Catherine reached the age of twelve, her parents expected her to follow the local custom that required women to marry at an early age, usually by fourteen. When they began to look for a suitable marriage partner for her, the ensuing conflict showed Catherine's determination and stubbornness, as well as the skills of persuasion she would later demonstrate in diplomatic assignments.

After several unsuccessful attempts to persuade Catherine to change her mind, her parents enlisted the help of Dominican friar Thomas della Fonte, a close family friend. He tried to convince Catherine to obey her parents and consent to marry, but Catherine persuaded him otherwise by reiterating the vow she had made to Christ. He then gave her a suggestion to help her cause: "Cut off all your hair and maybe that will stop them."[8] Catherine happily took his advice, much to the frustration of her parents.

In desperation, Catherine's parents instigated a plan calculated to force her to change her mind: They heaped many demanding tasks on her so she would have no time for her private devotions. But Catherine was not deterred. She built a private inner cell to which she could retreat and cheerfully performed all the kitchen-maid duties imposed on her. Eventually, her family gave in, and Catherine moved ahead with her plans.

At that time there were no cloistered religious institutions for women in Siena, but Catherine was inspired by a group of Sienese women known as the Mantellate, who belonged to the Third Order of St. Dominic. They were not nuns but rather lay women who lived in their own homes and held regular meetings in the chapel of San Domenico. These women served the sick and poor of Siena, and Catherine was determined to join them.

Initially, the group objected to Catherine because she

seemed too young and inexperienced. But her persistence and spiritual maturity overcame their resistance, and they finally admitted her. In 1363, at the age of sixteen, Catherine formally took on the white habit, the black mantle, and the white coif of the Mantellate and settled into what she thought was to be her spiritual life. She secluded herself, praying and fasting in the silence of her "cell," a small room in her parents' home. Turning her back on "worldly delights," she set her heart on the object of her desire, the Lord Jesus Christ.

Spiritual Crisis

Three years later, however, Catherine faced a spiritual crisis that ended her life of seclusion and plunged her into the world. Her biographer tells us that Catherine heard the "urgent voice" of the Lord "calling her to leave sweet rest for toil, the silence of her solitude for turmoil, the cloistered quiet of her cell for the busy throngs of men." She could no longer keep her brilliant light hidden under a bushel. She was told to "fulfill all justice," not just for herself but for others as well. But Catherine protested that she had just freed herself from temporal cares: "How can I put on again what I have cast off?"[9]

Furthermore, Catherine protested that her sex "puts many obstacles in the way. The world has no use for women in such work as that, and propriety forbids a woman to mix so freely in the company of men." God reminded her that nothing is impossible with the One who created both male and female. "Does it not depend on my own will where I shall pour out my grace? With me there is no longer male and female, nor lower class and upper class; for all stand equal in my sight, and all things are equally in my power to do."[10]

Ultimately, Catherine left her cell and began to perform "shining deeds of charity" toward her neighbors.[11] As her reputation for holiness grew through her acts of mercy and miraculous conversions of sinners, so did the circle of friends who became her spiritual family. Her expanding contacts introduced her to the politics of her city and the conflicts facing the Church. It was during this time that the politically astute Dominican friar Raymond of Capua became Catherine's spiritual director, and he kept her informed of political events.

In late medieval Italy, there was no separation of church and state. People viewed the world through Christianity-colored glasses. There was no separation of spiritual goals from secular interests. The spears and swords of opposing groups were thrust in the name of religion as well as of government.

In Siena, plots and counterplots, torture and executions were the order of the day. When a group called Party of the Nine was in control of government, rival insurgents overthrew them and established a government of the Twelve. To add to the tumult, powerful bands of armed mercenaries, such as John Hawkwood and the White Company, who could be hired by any group with enough money, stormed through Italian cities, plundering and slaying as they went. Needless to say, citizens lived in a constant state of fear and insecurity.

Dissention, violence and scandal damaged the lives of religious and clergy as well. A Sienese chronicler reports that "friars fought with knives, and fourteen were killed;" a provincial at another convent was murdered and "every convent divided against itself." Darkness reigned both inside and outside religious communities.[12]

Catherine Enters the Fray

Motivated by a need to respond to these conditions, Catherine could no longer keep silent. She entered the fray with the tools available to her: the spoken and written word. As Suzanne Noffke tells us, Catherine was a woman of her time "when the structures and authority of the Church as religious institution were quite universally accepted as a given."[13] She believed that the Church is "Christ on earth," and her response to the violence was to stress obedience to the pope. In the nearly four-hundred letters Catherine wrote during her life, she consistently demanded faithfulness to the truth as she saw it. For her that meant truth based on the Christian ideal of love and justice. When she boldly admonished King Charles V of France for "pretending not to see" abuses committed by his staff, she reminded him that God was the source of his authority. As king, he was responsible when the poor were denied justice in the courts. "The poor, whose crimes aren't one-thousandth as serious [as those of the rich], are punished without mercy."[14] Furthermore, Catherine insisted that justice without mercy is injustice.

Ultimately, news of Catherine's holiness and growing influence reached Pope Gregory XI at the papal palace, which at that time was in Avignon, not in Rome. The pope sent a messenger to ask for her prayers for himself and for the Church.

Political and social conditions in Rome had forced Pope Clement V to move the papacy to Avignon. Forty-four years before Catherine's birth, a conflict had erupted between Pope Boniface VIII and King Philip IV of France in 1303. The issue focused on who had the power to levy taxes and who paid the taxes. When the king levied taxes on clerical income without permission from the pope, Boniface responded by forbidding the clergy to pay these taxes. In a tit-for-tat move, Philip called on his council to judge the pope on trumped up charges of murder and heresy. In retaliation, the pope prepared to excommunicate the king, but the king's agents blocked the move by seizing the pope at his summer home in Anagni near Rome.

Later, a Frenchman was elected Pope Clement V. Fearful of Italian revenge for the crime against Boniface, he established a temporary papacy in Avignon near the Rhone River. "Temporary" lasted through six French popes, and the seat of the papacy resided in Avignon from 1309 to 1377.

Historian Barbara Tuchman describes the palace at Avignon as a place of "sumptuous pomp." The exterior was built fortress style with battlements and twelve-foot-thick walls for defense. Its splendid interior was decked out royally with elegant furnishings of gold and silver and hangings of silk. Of the prelates themselves, the poet Petrarch wrote that they ride on horses "decked in gold, fed on gold, soon to be shod in gold if the Lord does not check this slavish luxury."[15]

Having lost the prestige it had in Rome and dominated by French power, the papacy became a revenue-producing institution, selling not only indulgences but everything from bishops' sees and cardinals' hats to legitimizing priests' children. St. Bridget of Sweden lamented, "All the words of the Ten Commandments have been gathered up into one, and that is: Bring hither the money!"[16]

News of the corruption had caught Catherine's attention, and in 1376 she wrote several letters to Pope Gregory XI, the last pope to reside in Avignon, urging him to clean up the corruption in the Church and return the papacy to Rome.

Catherine's Mission

Here Catherine stood—one woman, one voice. Yet she had an indelible impact on the politics of her time. The pope not only responded to her letters, but would soon receive her as an ambassador for peace.

Others as well were turning to Catherine for help, including the leaders of Florence. This city had led a league of Italian cities in a war against the papacy, and in return, the pope had imposed an interdict that had devastating effects on Florence's economy. The interdict allowed other cities to refuse to trade with Florentines or pay debts owed to them. Their galleys could be captured, and they were denied any assistance from other Christians. Raymond of Capua wrote, "In all the world, Florentines were seized and deprived of their property by the government of the country in which they carried on their trade."[17]

In the end, the Florentines were forced to negotiate peace with the pope. Knowing of Catherine's reputation as a peacemaker, and that she had the ear of the pope, they asked her to mediate for them.

Thus, this courageous woman, devoted to Christ, who had intended to live a life of prayer and penance, moved out onto the medieval world stage. In May of 1376, Catherine accepted the diplomatic mission and started out on her long journey to the papal palace in Avignon.

Chapter 5
A CONFRONTATION WITH THE POPE

Catherine and a small group of her friends left Florence in late May of 1376 and journeyed north by road. No details have been recorded about their overland trip, but we do know that during the last part of their journey a small ship carried them up the Rhone River. As they made their way upriver, between banks of green meadows and shimmering poplars, they could see the impressive spires and towers of Avignon, where the pope's castle loomed above a heavily fortified wall.

When Catherine and her companions arrived in Avignon on June 18, Raymond of Capua, who would act as her interpreter, greeted Catherine at the landing. Two days after her arrival, this humble dyer's daughter from Siena stood face-to-face with the "Viceregent of Christ," Pope Gregory XI.

Gregory has been described as pious and sincere, but weak and vacillating in his efforts to reform the Church and move the papacy back to Rome. Catherine lost no time in speaking straightforwardly. With Raymond translating her native Tuscan into Latin for the pope, she presented her case supporting peace with the Florentines. She urged the pope to remove the ecclesiastical censures against them. The pope responded by saying that he left the whole matter in Catherine's hands, but warned her "do not forget the dignity of the Church."[1]

Can you imagine this happening in our century—leaving the whole matter in a woman's hands? As astounding as this was, however, things did not go smoothly for Catherine. For starters, the three Florentine ambassadors who were supposed to arrange peace terms did not show up.

Typical of the times, a new government had taken over in Florence between the time Catherine had left Florence and the time she met with the pope. The new Signoria were divided among themselves over whether they really wanted peace with the papacy. Upon hearing that the Florentines had levied a new tax on the clergy, Catherine wrote a letter reproaching them for their "rash increase of taxes."[2] She warned that they put the peace process in jeopardy and inquired as to why their envoys had not come yet. However, she reassured them that they would be received in a spirit of peace when they did arrive.

Yet when the Florentines finally arrived, they refused to negotiate with Catherine. They told her they had no orders to confer with her and were not interested in the peace terms arranged between her and the previous government. Nonetheless, in spite of their opposition, Catherine continued to intercede on their behalf with the pope. But the Florentines had not come in good faith. Negotiations with the cardinals appointed as mediators by the pope broke down, and the Florentines left Avignon without a peace agreement.

We get some insight into Catherine's spirit in her response to this setback. Instead of taking the Florentines' rebuff personally, she redirected her time in Avignon to what she had long held to be a higher mission: She urged the pope to return the papacy to Rome and to reform the Church. Rome had long been the traditional site of the papacy because Saints Peter and Paul were believed to have been martyred and buried there. Addressing the corruption surrounding the papacy, Catherine spoke so boldly to the pope about the "shameful vices of the Roman Curia" that her interpreter, Raymond, became uncomfortable. But, amazingly, the pope listened.[3]

The Turning Point

Catherine was well aware of proper women's behavior in fourteenth-century Italy, and especially as it concerned speaking to the pope. For his part, Gregory followed protocol required by the times regarding her status and his as well. In this light, one conversation in particular is worth quoting. When the pope asked Catherine for advice about returning to Rome, she replied: "It is not meet that a wretched little woman should give advice to the Sovereign Pontiff." The pope responded: "I do not ask you for advice, but to tell me the will of God in this matter."[4] Catherine continued to resist until the pope insisted under the command of obedience that she tell him "if she knew anything of the will of God in this affair."[5] She did know. Once past the required formalities, in other words, they got down to business.

Catherine reminded the pope of the vow he had made as a cardinal to return the papacy to Rome. Chroniclers relate that the pope was stunned by her remark because he had never told a soul of his vow. This conversation was a turning point. The pope knew from then on that he would have to leave Avignon and return to Rome. But he was also well aware of the strength of the opposition he faced.

Catherine's growing influence with the pope did not go unnoticed by the members of the papal court. Three members of the Curia made an attempt to discredit her in an "inquisition" approved by the pope. But their efforts failed. Catherine's wise, thoughtful answers to questions designed to trip her up won over her questioners. After she was cleared of heresy, the pope told her that if they bothered her again, "she had only to close the door in their faces."[6]

The French cardinals, however, remained political enemies of Catherine because they opposed the pope's leaving Avignon.

As Gregory prepared for his move to Rome, which required twenty-two galleys and smaller ships to meet his party at Marseilles, he faced increasing obstacles from the Frenchmen. The King of France, Charles V, sent his brother, the Duke of Anjou, to attempt to prevent Gregory's move. This show of power once again rallied all but one of the cardinals to oppose the pope's move back to Rome.

The cardinals continued to hammer away at the pope's decision. In the face of this unremitting opposition—adding to his own fear of hurting his family and friends—Gregory began to waver. He sent messages via Raymond of Capua to Catherine expressing his misgivings about moving to Rome.

Once again we gain a clue into Catherine's keen understanding of how politics worked. She knew that the influence of her previous conversations with the pope was fading under the pressure of the cardinals and the French king. She countered by sending the pope a number of letters, addressing every objection the French cardinals made to the move.

Still wavering, Gregory found what he thought to be a perfect justification to defend reconsidering his decision. He told Catherine that Pope Clement IV never took any action without the advice of the College of Cardinals and always followed their decisions, even if their opinion was contrary to his own. Catherine wisely responded: "Alas, most holy Father, these men quote Pope Clement IV to you, but they tell you nothing about Pope Urban V, who asked their advice about things when he was in doubt whether it was better to do them or not; but when a thing was absolutely clear to him, as your going is to you (about which you are certain), he took no heed of their counsel, but followed his own, and did not care although they were all against him."[7]

With steadfast persistence, Catherine continued to urge Gregory to put reform of the Church and the care of souls ahead of objections from those whose motives were based on the desire for status and pleasure. Always a pragmatist, she knew that constant pressure from the cardinals would cause the pope to delay his departure from Avignon, as he had done once before. So she gave him shrewd, practical advice: "Adopt a holy deception; let it seem that you are going to delay for a time and then do it swiftly and suddenly, for the more quickly it is done, the sooner will you be freed from these torments and troubles."[8]

We can admire not only her political acumen but also her understanding of human longings and shortcomings. Catherine told the pope that he was a wise man and would not succumb to snares again.

But the French cardinals were not about to be defeated. They connived to get a person reputed to be a saint to send a letter to the pope, warning the pope that if he went to Rome he would be poisoned. Hesitating over his decision yet again, the pope sent the letter on to Catherine. She questioned the authorship of the letter and called it "the work of a devil in human shape." She told him that a true "servant of God" would not use the risk of danger to discourage a good action.[9]

Here we get a glimpse into her astute argumentation: She pointed out that poison could be bought in Avignon as well as in Rome. Once more she urged the pope to go without fear, reminding him that she prayed for him often.

The Pope Makes His Move

On September 13, 1376, just three months after Catherine's initial meeting with the pope, Gregory left the papal palace to begin the journey to Rome. He had finally taken Catherine's advice, announcing his intention to the cardinals and departing suddenly. Johannes Jorgensen describes the scene: "In vain did the French cardinals burst into tears, in vain did Gregory's father, old Count Guillaume de Beaufort, throw himself down on the threshold and implore his son to stay."[10] Gregory stepped over the prostrate body of his father and left Avignon.

The papal party arrived in Marseilles on September 20, but at the last minute the thought of leaving France forever caused Gregory to hesitate yet one more time. Finally, on October 2, the pope and his retinue, with reluctance and more tears, boarded the galley that was to take them from France on to Genoa.

On the same day the pope left Avignon, Catherine and her companions started their overland journey back to her hometown of Siena, Italy. However, Catherine's companions fell ill, and their journey was delayed. In a fateful coincidence, they were still in Genoa when the pope arrived.

Stormy seas had buffeted the papal ships as they moved along the Riviera, forcing the fleet to sail into ports along the way. The gale-force winds had shaken the pope, and the cardinals called the bad weather a divine omen warning them that they should not continue on to Rome.

When they finally reached Genoa on October 18, they received disturbing political news: Rome was in turmoil. The Florentines were winning battles against papal troops in the northern and eastern areas of the region. The bad political news, along with the experience of near shipwreck, gave the cardinals the ammunition they needed. They were determined to use these events to pressure the pope to return once again to Avignon. A consistory of cardinals, presided over by the pope, was convened and a majority of the cardinals voted to go back to Avignon.

A Secret Meeting

Just as Gregory was on the verge of going along with the cardinals' decision, he hesitated. He had heard Catherine was in town and wanted to talk with her. Jorgensen suggests that the pope may have thought he had enough reasons to persuade Catherine to agree to his return to Avignon and thus ease his conscience.

But arranging a meeting posed several problems, especially since the pope knew the cardinals would raise stiff opposition.[11] Gregory also thought it would be beneath his dignity—even cause a scandal—to meet Catherine in public among the throngs of people who followed her wherever she went.

So the pope arranged to meet Catherine secretly at night in the home of a noble lady, Orietta Scotti, where Catherine was staying. Disguising himself in the dress of an ordinary priest, the pope went to the Palazzo Scotti without an escort and asked to see Catherine. "Catherine fell at his feet; he bade her rise, for he himself was a suppliant and besought her to obtain him the grace to know what course he should adopt. After a long colloquy with her, Gregory departed, full of edification and with his courage restored."[12]

The meeting of Catherine and the pope was a fateful one for the Church. Catherine's powers of persuasion must have been very convincing, because Gregory immediately informed the cardinals of his determination to continue on to Rome. He ordered the fleet ready, and on October 29 they set sail. Yet even after the pope left, Catherine's influence did not wane. Though she remained in Genoa because of the outbreak of illness among her companions, Catherine continued writing to Gregory. Ever mindful of the pope's tendency to vacillate, she faithfully bolstered his courage.

The pope's journey was not an easy one. The dangerous storms they had previously encountered continued to buffet them, sinking two of the papal galleys. Although no lives were lost, the pope found it necessary to allay the fears of the cardinals. He urged them to "take heart," saying that the tempests "were the sign of a great victory and no prince had ever come to Italy without enduring storms and tribulations at sea if he were afterwards to prove a conqueror, as was shown by the example of Aeneas and King Charles."[13]

Finally, on December 5, 1376, the papal party reached the shores of the Papal States at the port of Corneto. On January 17, 1377, a cheering crowd met Gregory in front of St. Paul's in Rome. Waving flowers and throwing confetti, they escorted him to the Vatican. By the light of torches, the Roman people danced through the night in celebration.[14]

Catherine's efforts to bring the pope back to Rome had

succeeded. But the joy of his return did not last. Fifteen months later, Pope Gregory XI was dead.

Chapter 6
SUCCESS IN FLORENCE, FAILURE IN ROME

After spending the summer of 1376 in Avignon, then surviving her companions' illness in Genoa, Catherine finally was able to leave for Siena. But her traveling party had more hurdles to cross: They, too, experienced dangerous storms at sea and nearly faced shipwreck. When they arrived safely in Siena by the end of December, her family and friends welcomed her with a joyful reunion.

It would seem they had plenty to celebrate—not only Catherine's safe return but also her accomplishment in persuading the pope to return to Rome. But terrible political news disheartened Catherine: Hostilities had erupted on several fronts. Fighting between factions of the powerful Sienese Salimbeni family threatened to plunge the entire area into civil war.[1] Renewed fighting between the Florentines and the pope killed hopes for a negotiated peace. Particularly distressing to Catherine was the fact that Siena had joined the antipapal league, led by the Florentines.

Catherine was a woman who yearned for peace. So it is no surprise that she energetically responded to requests for help in negotiating disputes between enemies. Catherine's idea of peacemaking meant " 'being with' both sides of a conflict and mediating their differences through direct speech."[2] Catherine felt that openness to truth demanded no less.

When she was asked to intervene in the Salimbeni dispute, Catherine once more entered the fray. She traveled to the fortress of Cione Salimbeni and then to that of Agnolino Salimbeni, the two warring parties. One can imagine her patiently addressing the grievances of both sides as she brought them to the point of halting hostilities. While no details of her negotiations have been recorded, the chronicler Francesco Malavolti reported that she was able to bring about an agreement "which many other barons and potent men" had been unable to achieve.[3] Given the turbulent tenor of the times, however, like most peace agreements this one was destined to be short-lived.

Larger battles demanded Catherine's attention. In early 1378, she received a command from Pope Gregory, via Raymond of Capua, to go to Florence to help negotiate a peace between the Holy See and the Florentine Republic. This diplomatic mission would both challenge Catherine's political skills and put her life in danger.

The conflict between Florence and the papacy had been building for quite some time, and both sides had committed outrages that fueled the fray. Florence felt threatened by the Church's control over the area in central Italy known as the Papal States. The Church, in turn, felt threatened by its loss of territory within the Papal States during the years the papacy resided in Avignon.

Things escalated during a food shortage when representatives prohibited shipment of food from the Papal States to Florence. Florence, in retaliation, organized a revolt against the pope. Both sides hired powerful mercenary armies to attack the other.

The situation worsened when Cardinal Robert of Geneva, who would later become known as the "Butcher of Cesena" and "Man of Blood," led the fight to regain control of the Papal States. Furious over the Florentines' victories, including their take-over of Bologna, a key Papal State, Cardinal Robert decided to target the town of Cesena in northeastern Italy to provoke fear in would-be rebels. His troops won that battle, but he was not content to stop there. In a horrifying strategy, he promised the citizens of Cesena leniency and persuaded the men to disarm themselves. Then he called in the English captain, John Hawkwood, and his mercenaries to join his forces and ordered them to slaughter the defenseless citizens of Cesena.

Though Hawkwood hesitated and offered a more merciful solution, the cardinal demanded "blood and more blood." Hawkwood obliged, though he later left the service of the Church because of Robert's brutality. Hawkwood's troops savagely killed thousands of people, including babies, causing the archbishop of St. Antonio to compare him with Herod and Nero.[4] There was enough blood on both sides to make the possibility of a peace agreement between the pope and the Florentine League remote at best.

Appalled at this violence, Catherine once more wrote the pope, urging him to make peace. She candidly pointed out that the Church had lost influence because it engaged in war and because of the corrupt actions of the clergy. Catherine advised the pope to appoint good men as rulers.[5]

However, hostilities continued. Florentine leaders decided to ignore the interdict the pope had imposed, and they levied new taxes on Church property. Eventually, both sides ran out of money, having squandered funds on mercenaries. This finally opened a window of opportunity for peace.

Around this time, Catherine's influential Florentine friend, Niccolo Soderini, gave Raymond of Capua a fateful message for the pope. Soderini claimed that the Florentines really wanted peace and that only a small faction of leaders stood in the way. He recommended negotiations with a coalition of Guelphic party leaders and citizens.[6]

The pope responded to the message by saying, "If Catherine of Siena went to Florence, peace would be made."[7] From this response, it is reasonable to speculate that Catherine's previous letters had made an impression on the pope. Because of dangerous conditions in Florence, however, Raymond offered to go in her place. But the pope objected, saying that Catherine would not likely be harmed because she was so revered.

Revered or not, her life would be threatened.

Ambassador for Peace

Catherine received credentials to go to Florence as the pope's ambassador for peace, and she departed in December of 1377 with a small escort of friends. In early 1378 she met with Niccolo Soderini and other officials of the Guelphic party in Florence to plan their strategy. It was during one of these meetings that Catherine made a painful political mistake—one that would result in serious consequences.

Perhaps out of her zeal for peace or uncharacteristic shortsightedness, Catherine sided with Guelphic party leaders who decided to banish from office those who wanted to prolong the war. She had not anticipated the consequences. Party extremists used her prestige and endorsement as cover for their plan to take revenge on personal enemies, which ended up increasing hostility between political factions in Florence.[8]

Meanwhile, at the urging of Catherine and Guelphic party officials, negotiations for a peace conference continued. Finally, in early March of 1378, a number of ambassadors representing the Florentine league and three representatives sent by the pope met in Sarzana. On March 22, 1378, a peace agreement was in sight. But tragedy struck before an agreement could be reached. On March 27, Pope Gregory died. When the papal representatives received the news, they left the conference without signing an agreement.

Once again we get a glimpse into Catherine's political astuteness. Instead of sitting idly by while things fell apart, Catherine took advantage of the opportunity presented by the pope's death. Since part of the tension was caused by the Florentines' refusal to obey Pope Gregory's interdict, Catherine urged them to show the new pope their sincere intention for peace by obeying the interdict. The Signoria of the governing council agreed, and Catherine saw the first "streaks of dawn" coming for peace.[9]

Yet once again Catherine's good work was foiled. On April 8, the conclave of cardinals elected a new pope, Urban VI, who would prove to be a problematic contrast to Pope Gregory XI. While Gregory was weak and vacillating, Urban was strong and stern. He began his pontificate with a do-or-die goal of reforming the Church, and his zealotry quickly made him harsh and uncompromising. "From a humble unspectacular official totally unprepared for the papal throne, he was transformed overnight into an implacable scourge of simony, moved less by religious zeal than by simple hatred and jealousy of privilege." Urban had no tact. He called one cardinal a half-wit and told another, "Shut your mouth!"[10]

Catherine received word of Urban's abrasive personality: "From what is being said, this new Holy Father is a terrible man and he fills people with terror by his manner and his words."[11] To add to the bad news, prospects for peace were dimmed when Urban said he would not accept the previous pope's terms of agreement with the Florentines.

Not one to relent in the face of obstacles, Catherine continued her pursuit of peace, sending a strong letter to Pope Urban addressing the issues as she saw them. She reminded the pope of the need to be "grounded in love" in the performance of his duties. She attacked the decay of the Church and the vices of the clergy. "They behave like drovers, they throw dice with their anointed hands, they sell the blood of Christ and spend the money on the children of their concubines."[12] Finally, she pleaded with the pope to forgive the Florentines, putting in a good word for them by saying they will prove themselves to be "better sons than all the others."[13]

Urban received Catherine's letter at a critical time. Threats were mounting to challenge the legitimacy of his election as pope, and he desperately needed a peace agreement with the Florentines. On July 18, the pope's messenger rode into Florence carrying an olive branch. Peace had finally come.

The great bells of the Cathedral and the Palazzo Vecchio rang out, and the people were jubilant. Catherine wrote of the news to friends in Siena and enclosed "a leaf of the blessed olive branch" in her letter.[14] The papal interdict against the Florentines was removed, and a peace agreement was signed on July 28, 1378.

Fracture in Rome

Despite a successful peace agreement with the Florentines, opposition to Pope Urban continued to grow, not only because of his harsh personality but also because of his somewhat questionable election. His enemies were all too happy to use the confusing circumstances of his election as an excuse to remove him.

When the previous pope died, the citizens of Rome had been worried that a French pope would move the papacy back to Avignon, so they demanded the election of a Roman pope. However, there were only two Roman cardinals, and neither was electable. One was too old and infirm; the other too young and inexperienced. In addition, reaching an agreement to elect one of the remaining cardinals seemed hopeless because of the rivalry between the French factions.

In the end, the cardinals chose a compromise candidate: Bartolomeo Prignano, Archbishop of Bari, an Italian but not a Roman. But it was not a successful compromise. The French cardinals considered him inferior and someone they could manipulate. And the Italians were not satisfied because he was not a Roman. Crowds gathered and demanded, *"Romano lo volemo!"* ("We want a Roman!").

Terrified of the mob, the cardinals devised a scheme to appease the crowd by dressing the elderly Roman Cardinal Tebaldeschi in papal robes and presenting him as pope. The placating gesture gave the cardinals enough time to escape to fortresses outside the city. But news of the fraud spread quickly, and the angry crowd shouted, "Death to the cardinals!"[15]

The next day the cardinals formally announced the election of the Archbishop of Bari as Pope Urban VI.

The illusion of compromise did not last long. By summer, the new pope's abusive treatment of the cardinals who elected him had become intolerable. The French cardinals held a secret meeting at the papal summer residence in Anagni to consider solutions. They focused their attention on the questionable April papal election and argued that the election was not valid because threats of mob violence had interfered with their free choice.

On August 9, 1378—just weeks after Urban had signed the Florentine peace agreement—thirteen cardinals published a declaration stating that the papal election of Urban VI was invalid and asked the pope to abdicate. Fearful of Roman retaliation, the cardinals then placed themselves under the military protection of the Count of Fondi.

Catherine had barely returned home from a successful mission in Florence when she learned of the terrible news unfolding in Rome. Believing she should have done more through prayers and letters to prevent the developing schism, Catherine felt such extreme sorrow and guilt over her inadequacy that she became ill. While staying at her sister-in-law's farm near Siena, she visited a nearby country church where she is said to have experienced a vision that gave her courage and zeal and renewed vigor.[16] Catherine was able to return home filled with energy—and ready to continue her fight for the unity of the Church.

A Grassroots Movement

Catherine's strengths were needed now more than ever. Politically savvy, she understood the need for grassroots action to make political change. Faced with the biggest political battle of her life, she sent letters to influential individuals, as well as many ordinary people, to convince them to support Urban as the lawful pope. Drawing on her considerable talents of persuasion, she dictated letters to three secretaries who wrote as fast as they could to keep up with her.

Catherine never wavered in her conviction that Urban was the true pope and that he had been legitimately elected. For her, the pope was "Christ on earth," and any challenge to the papacy was a threat to the unity of the Church. Her vigorous response to the developing disaster was never more pronounced than in her letter to three wavering Italian cardinals who had not decided for or against Pope Urban. One gets the impression that Catherine used every image she could think of in her verbal scathing to add persuasiveness to her argument.

First, she reminded them that they knew very well that they had followed the rules when they elected Urban, and that it was only Roman threats that influenced their decision after the election. She rebuked them as "wretched and cowardly knights. Your shadow has made you afraid." She argued that their actions would shred faith and spread darkness among the faithful: "You are not flowers that emit a fragrance but a stench that has caused the whole world to reek." With building intensity, she scolded: "Ah, you fools, worthy of a thousand deaths! Like blind men, you do not see your own evil. You have come to such confusion that you have become liars and idolaters."[17]

While it is impossible to know for certain what effect her letter had on the cardinals, it is interesting to note that later, when the French cardinals elected Clement as pope, the three Italian cardinals abstained from voting.

During the three months Catherine remained in Siena, her health rapidly deteriorated, and she sensed that her life would soon end. She felt depressed over the developing crisis in the Church, and she wanted to leave a spiritual legacy for her followers. It was during this period that Catherine wrote her book, *The Dialogue*, a mystical treatise based on "conversations" she had with God. She "recorded the truth as revealed by the Godhead to her in the ecstasy of her soul, which truth she had been warned not to keep for herself but to share with others."[18]

On September 20, 1378, the conclave of cardinals, in opposition to Pope Urban, met in Fondi and elected Robert of Geneva as the rival Pope Clement VII. One has to wonder what the cardinals were thinking. They elected the former "butcher of Cesena"! Perhaps they were swayed by the fact that Robert was related to the French royal family and had other impressive connections. Whatever their motives, the decision caused the Great Western Schism, pitting one pope against another, a division that split the Church and society into two hostile camps for the next forty years.

The battle lines had been drawn. King Charles V of France supported Pope Clement, who had moved his rival papacy to Avignon, and the king demanded loyalty toward the new rival pope from his subjects. England, at war with France, continued to support Pope Urban. And so it went, with countries lining up on one side or the other. Leaders fought each other—and sometimes their own people—over which pope deserved allegiance. To add to the misery, each pope excommunicated the other and all his followers, thus creating widespread fear of damnation among the faithful.

From our twenty-first century perspective, it is difficult to imagine the full effects of the schism. It ultimately shook up all aspects of fourteenth-century life and eventually led to more war, as the rival popes hired armies and rulers and subjects were forced to take sides.

Called to Rome

Even though Catherine had predicted the schism, the news that Clement had been elected nearly broke her heart. "It is a time for weeping," she lamented.[19] But she had enough of words. Catherine wanted to be in the midst of events, on the "field of battle," and fight for the cause of truth.[20] When the summons came from Pope Urban to go to Rome, she was ready. In early November, with a large company of friends, Catherine left for Rome, never to return to Siena.

It is interesting to note that, before she left Siena, Catherine asked Raymond to obtain a written order from the pope for her travel to Rome. As a dedicated virgin, she was supposed to stay put in her cell and do good quietly. Catherine must have grown weary of the gossip that circulated among the townspeople every time she traveled somewhere. This time she received an official order from Pope Urban requiring her to go to Rome under obedience to him.

When Catherine and her friends arrived in Rome on November 28, Pope Urban had a full workload waiting for her. First, he asked her to speak to the assembly of his new cardinals. Catherine urged the cardinals to be courageous and not be frightened by the schism. She encouraged them to continue working for God and to put their faith in divine providence. Her address was so uplifting that the pope said her courage put them all to shame.[21]

Pope Urban needed Catherine's help on one front in particular. Queen Joanna of Naples was a supporter of the rival Pope Clement and provided a base for him in Italy. Pope Urban badly needed to change Joanna's mind and earn her support, and he thought perhaps Catherine could persuade her. But when told of possible danger to Catherine at the queen's court, the pope withdrew his order for her to go. Catherine, fearless as she was, complained, "These are vain considerations, which proceed from lack of faith rather than from true prudence."[22]

True to character, Catherine was determined to persuade the queen, and sent a letter warning the queen that her support of Clement would cause division among her subjects and weaken her authority.[23] Catherine further forewarned the queen that her life was in danger because of political intrigue within her kingdom. Joanna responded immediately, announcing that she acknowledged Urban as the true pope—even though she later would rescind her statement. Unfortunately, Catherine's predictions about danger later came true when the queen was found murdered in her bed.

Catherine kept faith even when the cause seemed hopeless. She tried to change the mind of King Charles V of France, who supported Clement because he wanted a French pope in Avignon. Catherine urged the king to heed the advice of the University of Paris, where scholars had recommended a Church council be held to determine which of the popes was valid. The fact that the French king subsequently silenced the theologians proved in a perverse way that her suggestion, if it had been taken, was sound.

Back on the home front, Catherine continued her attempts to strengthen Pope Urban's position by urging him to gather his supporters. The pope listened to Catherine's advice and sent out a papal bull to neighboring spiritual leaders, summoning them to his side. Catherine's powerful influence is seen even here in the details. For example, along with the papal document the pope chose to include a letter from Catherine urging these spiritual leaders to come at once.

The Last Battle

At the same time tensions were mounting over who was to be the spiritual leader of the Church, tension was also growing between the pope and the Roman people. This was to be Catherine's last political battle. Catherine had urged the pope to meet the leaders of the city as equals and "receive them with the greatest possible friendliness." It is believed that because of Catherine's influence on the leader of the Roman republicans, Giovanni Cenci, violence was avoided and the two sides were reconciled.[24]

While Catherine was helping to build support for the pope, her own physical condition was rapidly deteriorating. A friend described her condition, saying that "the skin rested on the bones without anything between. Her stomach no longer received any food and she could not even swallow a refreshing drink of water."[25] Catherine is thought to have had a stroke on January 30, 1380, becoming partially paralyzed. The stroke, as well as the stress of many battles and her severe ascetic practices, had taken their toll.

A threat on Pope Urban's life was the final blow that brought about Catherine's death. She spent her last days in a home near St. Peter's, praying constantly. Despite intense pain, she spoke with disciples who visited her and wrote a loving farewell to her dear friend Raymond of Capua. Catherine died at age thirty-three on Sunday, April 29, 1380, with her mother and her companions at her side.

The Great Western Schism was to last for another thirty-eight years. After Catherine's death, Pope Urban is said to have become a ruthless tyrant, hated by all. Perhaps if Catherine had lived longer, she may have been able to shorten the schism. She might have had a moderating influence on the harsh personality of Urban, as she had advised him earlier to deal gently with people rather than "by force or with harsh words."[26]

This amazing woman, Catherine of Siena, an Italian mystic and diplomat and an extraordinary envoy, actively influenced the church and secular politics of her time. She urged those in authority to use their power for the good of their subjects, and she fought hard to negotiate peace and bring about reconciliation between warring groups. By persuading Pope Gregory XI to move the papacy back to Rome, she played a significant role in shaping the future history of Christianity.

Catherine was canonized a saint in 1461 by Pope Pius II. On October 4, 1970, Pope Paul VI proclaimed her a Doctor of the Church, one week after St. Teresa of Avila received the same honor. It is of note that prior to 1970 this title had never been conferred on any woman. Six-hundred years after her death, Catherine was still breaking barriers for women, just as she had done all her short life. The pope called her "The Doctor of Unity."

III

ST. TERESA OF AVILA

Reformer

"Saint Teresa" by Francois Gerard (1770-1837). Oil on canvas, 172 x 96 cm.
Photo Credit: Erich Lessing / Art Resource, NY
Maison Marie-Therese, Paris, France

Chapter 7
TAINTED BLOOD

Two days after they began a life of prayer and poverty in a new Carmelite convent, four nuns found themselves under attack by the townspeople of Avila, Spain. Local opposition to the opening of St. Joseph's had rapidly developed into an all-out protest. Shouting abuse, councilmen "hammered on the doors, but the nuns reinforced them with wooden beams and the locks held."[1] Thus began the first of Teresa of Avila's seventeen convents in 1562, and the first of many battles she fought to achieve her reforms.

Teresa de Cepeda y Ahumada was born in Avila, Spain on March 28, 1515, the third of ten children of Alonso de Cepeda and his second wife, Beatriz de Ahumada. Teresa was considered attractive, of medium height with a round face, dark expressive eyes, and black hair. Biographers have described her as intelligent, charming, vivacious and witty, qualities she put to good use in the battles she fought in later life. Her well-to-do family had worked hard to acquire the status of minor nobility and fend off the rumors of unrespectable ancestry.

Status was of crucial importance in sixteenth-century

Spain. While older, established Christians had status, "New Christians," or converts, were viewed with suspicion. This bias dated back to 1478, when Pope Sixtus IV granted Spanish kings the right to set up Inquisition tribunals to deal with the problems of unorthodox teaching and *conversos*, Jewish converts. To protect themselves from anti-Semitism, many Jews had converted to Catholicism, and these "New Christians" were especially suspect.

In 1485, Tomás de Torquemada, inquisitor-general of the Spanish kingdom, established a tribunal in Toledo, the hometown of Teresa's paternal grandfather, Juan Sanchez. Agents of the Inquisition were sent to spy on "New Christians," and any evidence of *judaizing* was met with cruel punishment. The Spanish Inquisition, with its punishments of torture, burning at the stake, and life imprisonment, has long stood at the top of history's list for horrific forms of repression and persecution.

The fear caused by these punishments must have been overwhelming to people such as Teresa's grandfather, a "New Christian" convert who was suspected of clinging to Judaism. So it is not surprising that when the Inquisitors offered a lesser punishment to *judaizers* who came forward and confessed their "crimes" Juan Sanchez accepted. The Inquisitors reasoned that they were offering people a chance to be "reconciled" to the Church. But first, the "confessors" had to participate in a public punishment spectacle known as an *auto da fe*, which means "act of faith."

Juan Sanchez, his wife and sons (including Alonso, Teresa's father) were forced to walk barefoot through the streets of Toledo, enduring public humiliation from hostile crowds shouting insults. They were made to wear the degrading yellow *sambenitos*, tunics, inscribed with the offenders' names and alleged shameful deeds, which were then publicly displayed in parish churches.[2]

A New Start

To escape the stigma of this disgrace, Juan later moved his family from Toledo to Avila to make a new life. Avila was a walled city of medieval fortresses and towers built to keep invaders out, high on the Castilian plateau, seventy miles northwest of Madrid. In Avila, Juan joined a kinsman in a lucrative silk and woolen trade and was able to build a reputation managing the finances of local dignitaries.[3]

However, moving to a new city and becoming wealthy was not enough to gain Juan social respectability. Spaniards at the time were obsessed with genealogy and honor, especially the honor of *limpieza de sangre*, purity of blood. It was honorable to be a pure-blooded "Old Christian," but a convert or "New

Christian" was reputed to have tainted blood. To avoid suspicion, Juan worked to establish an "Old Christian" pedigree for himself and his family. He was wealthy enough to purchase a certificate testifying that he was a Spanish nobleman, and he made certain that his children chose marriage partners from "Old Christian" ancestry.

Teresa's father, Alonso Sanchez de Cepeda, inherited the nobility status of *hidalgo* purchased by his father. But it still was not enough to ensure his status. At the time, people of noble descent were not required to pay taxes as commoners were. However, some zealous tax collectors dug up witnesses who agreed to testify that Alonso's pedigree was false. The accusation threatened to expose the humiliation the Sanchez family had suffered in Toledo. Even though the case was eventually resolved in Alonso's favor, the continued threats against the family honor certainly had an impact on young, impressionable Teresa.[4] Would they be forced to undergo public disgrace and hostility again?

In her autobiography, Teresa wrote that her parents were "virtuous and God-fearing." She described her father as a man "very charitable with the poor" and stressed that he did not keep slaves, although it was common to do so at the time. She portrayed her mother, Beatriz de Ahumada, as a devoted mother who taught her children to say their prayers and encouraged their devotion to the Blessed Virgin.[5]

Teresa also wrote that she had a "great affection" for her sisters and brothers and that they read the lives of the saints together. She was particularly struck by the fact that some saints gained the great blessings of heaven through martyrdom. At age seven, Teresa and her favorite older brother, Rodrigo, decided on a plan to go to the land of the Moors, announce themselves Christians, get beheaded, and go straight to heaven. Fortunately, they were stopped on the way by a worried uncle looking for them.

Since martyrdom was unlikely, Teresa found other ways to imitate the lives of the saints. She and her brother decided to become hermits and built hermitages by piling up "heaps of small stones." With other young girls she would "build convents" and pretend they were nuns, with Teresa leading the way.[6]

When Teresa was thirteen, her mother died. This came at a vulnerable time for Teresa, who was beginning to experiment with her appearance, read books of romance and chivalry, and socialize with visiting relatives. She wrote of one association with a cousin where they engaged in "conversations and vanities," which she considered to be dangerous for her soul. She did not give details, but of one particular temptation she wrote, "This friendship pained my father and sister."[7]

Recognizing the potential danger to his daughter's reputation—and to his family's honor—Teresa's father decided to send her to Our Lady of Grace, a convent boarding school in Avila. There she could complete her education under supervision. After a fearful first week spent wondering what people had heard about her, Teresa settled down in the tranquil convent atmosphere. Surrounded by nuns with whom she quickly made friends, Teresa listened intently to the "good and holy conversation" of the novice mistress, Sister Maria. She later credited this saintly nun's good influence with helping her to "get rid of the habits that the bad company had caused and to turn my mind to the desire for eternal things."[8]

A year and a half later, Teresa left the convent school without a clear decision about her future. She had considered becoming a nun but was put off by the comments of some of the young sisters. They made it clear that convent life at Our Lady of Grace was "too severe and made excessive demands on them."[9] She was equally reluctant to marry, mindful of her mother's constant childbearing and subsequent early death. Unable to decide about her future, Teresa became ill and made plans to return home.

Teresa took advantage of her half-sister's offer to spend some time at her country home to recuperate. On the way she visited her devout Uncle Pedro, and the meeting proved providential for Teresa. Sensitive to her inner conflict, Pedro gave her a book of letters of St. Jerome to read. Living in Avila of the Knights, a city with a proud tradition of serving Spain on the battlefield, watching her brothers leave for war, and having attempted a journey to martyrdom herself, Teresa must have taken St. Jerome's words to heart: "Say, craven knight, what dost thou lingering there in thy father's house?"[10]

After more agonizing and illness, Teresa made her decision.

A Difficult Choice

Teresa's announcement to her father about her intention to become a nun brought them into painful conflict. Alonso objected strongly. Recently widowed, he did not want to lose his favorite daughter permanently, and he told her she could enter a convent over his dead body.

But Teresa was determined, and one morning in 1536, accompanied by her brother Rodrigo, she secretly escaped to the Carmelite Convent of the Incarnation. Her father was heartbroken, and Teresa suffered as well: "It seemed that every bone in my body was being sundered."[11] Eventually, her father came to accept her decision. As historian Stephen Clissold suggests, he must have recognized that his daughter had "inherited all the indomitable spirit of her grandfather, Juan Sanchez." In an about face, Alonso contributed a dowry of grain and gold to the convent, as well as personal items for his daughter.[12]

Incarnation Convent, built on an old Jewish cemetery outside the city walls, housed a mix of poor and wealthy women. The poor were housed in a common dormitory, while each of the wealthy nuns had her own suite of rooms. Since she came from a family of some means, Teresa enjoyed her own private apartment, which included a guest room to entertain visitors. Years later when she initiated her reforms, Teresa would do away with these class-based distinctions and privileges.

Teresa embraced convent life with a single-minded devotion and spiritedly wrote that God had given her "great happiness" in the religious life. But changes in her habits and diet, along with her overly conscientious effort to overcome her "evil deeds," caused fainting fits and fever.[13] Doctors diagnosed a variety of ailments, including heart disease and palsy, but were unable to affect a cure. Alarmed over her condition, Teresa's father took her out of the convent and sent her to a healer in Becedas.[14]

On the way to Becedas, Teresa again stopped to visit her Uncle Pedro. This time he gave her a book that made a deep impression on her and profoundly affected her spiritual life. *The Third Spiritual Alphabet* by Franciscan Friar Francis de Osuna described the step-by-step technique of "mental prayer" that started with recollecting the senses, focusing within, and detaching oneself from external distractions. Teresa took to it like a fish to water. She believed it was just what she needed to learn how to "proceed in prayer" and to build a personal relationship with God.[15]

Heresy or Holiness?

When Teresa's health deteriorated because of the "barbarous ministrations" of the healer at Becedas, her father took her back home. Unfortunately, her health continued to deteriorate until she fell into a catatonic state.[16] Four days later, she inexplicably opened her eyes, and the Carmelite nuns carried her back to Incarnation Convent. It would take another three years in the convent infirmary before she fully recovered, a healing that she attributed to the intercession of St. Joseph.

It was customary under the relaxed Carmelite rule in those days for both men and women to visit nuns at the convent, and Teresa was particularly sought after for her spiritual advice and witty, charming conversation. She faced these increasing demands with renewed strength, but the time spent socializing took its toll, crowding out time for recollection and prayer.[17]

Beset by inner turmoil, Teresa continued to pray. Sometime around 1554, she wrote that she began to experience divine locutions, "inner voices," which she interpreted as Christ guiding and encouraging her. Although these new phenomena in her spiritual life were joyful experiences, they also brought some fear and anxiety. Were they from God or from the devil?

Christian Spain at the time considered any experience that challenged orthodoxy suspect. Growing as a dominant European power, Spain had anointed itself as the "defender of Catholic orthodoxy in a religiously divided Europe."[18] Increasingly repressive measures against "heretics" were carried out by the Office of the Inquisition. Officials were on the lookout for any sign of suspicious behavior that might be heretical, such as mystical experiences or individuals advocating mental prayer or contemplation. Given the repressive conditions of her society, it's no wonder that Teresa tried—unsuccessfully—to dismiss her experiences from her mind.[19]

An independent thinker devoted to mental prayer, Teresa found herself at odds with officially approved religious thought and practices of her day. Good Christians of the time were expected to participate in the formal rituals established by the Church, and experiencing God through mental prayer was branded a challenge to Church authority. Until Teresa matured enough to have confidence in her own ideas and experiences, these contradictory beliefs troubled her.

In an attempt to understand her experiences, Teresa sought out *letrados,* learned men, to give her feedback on the state of her soul. Early counselors Francis de Salcedo and Gaspar Daza proved too inexperienced and discouraging to help the spiritually gifted Teresa. They told her she was "suffering delusions."[20] Their unsympathetic response is understandable, given the fact that the Inquisition was looking over everyone's shoulder for evidence of *alumbrado* heresies. *Alumbrados* and *illuminati* were the names given to those who practiced mental prayer, studied scripture on their own, and claimed to act under the illumination of the Holy Spirit. It is reasonable to assume that Teresa's counselors were trying to protect her, as well as themselves, from accusations of heresy and subsequent punishment.

Thinking that others could be more helpful to Teresa—or relieving themselves of the responsibility—Salcedo and Daza recommended that Teresa contact the Jesuits at the new College of San Gil. It turned out to be good advice. There she found many learned men and met members of Avila's reform movement.[21]

The vice-rector of San Gil, Father Juan de Padranos, became Teresa's new confessor. Padranos' gentle guidance set Teresa's soul free, which led to new mystical experiences and to her first grace of ecstasy. Teresa described these powerful spiritual experiences variously as raptures, visions or locutions.

When Padranos fell ill, he was replaced by Father Baltasar Alvarez, who had to grow into the job of guiding Teresa. At first, his response to her mystical experiences was that she should "avoid too much solitude" and "seek distractions." He questioned Teresa at length, asking how she knew it was Jesus Christ present in her soul. Teresa struggled to answer, saying she did not know how he got there, only that it was so. Alvarez remained doubtful and was suspicious that Teresa was possessed.

But a short time later, Alvarez himself experienced a vision of Christ. When he told Teresa about it, she turned the tables on him, questioning how *he* knew his experience was valid. Alvarez argued his case and assured her he was not mistaken. Teresa replied, "Now you see, Father. This is how it appears to you. But to others it may appear to be whatever they say it is."[22] From then on, Alvarez accepted Teresa's experiences as authentic signs of holiness.

A Divine Mission

In 1560, when she was forty-five years old, Teresa wrote that she experienced a vision that would change the direction of her life. While praying one day, she had "seemingly been put in hell" where she felt herself "burning and crumbling." The "unbearable pain" so tormented her that, even years later, she suffered whenever she remembered the experience. When she recovered, she vowed to serve God by saving as many souls as she could from this everlasting torment.[23]

Even before this experience of hell, Teresa had been feeling restless and wanted to do more for God. This restlessness reflected the calls for reform that swept Spain during Teresa's time. Spain served as a leading example of Church reform throughout Christendom. For many religious leaders the practice of Christianity had deteriorated to a concern for accumulating wealth and property rather than a concern for the spiritual lives of their flocks. As a result, they had lost their moral authority, and calls for reform from the faithful grew widespread. Throughout Spain, "reform came to symbolize undefined longings for change within the ecclesiastical structure and for more spiritual solutions to problems."[24] By the early sixteenth century, Avila had become a center of religious fervor and reform movements. It is not surprising that Teresa and her friends at Incarnation Convent were affected by these reforms.

An idea came to Teresa one evening as she and a few friends were reflecting on a return to true poverty, the importance of prayer, and strict reclusion. Teresa had been inspired by the Discalced (Reformed) Franciscan Friars founded by Peter of Alcantara. "Discalced," which meant going barefoot or wearing sandals of woven rope, symbolized a life of radical poverty and penitence. Teresa was moved by the example of holiness and dedication to Christian ideals that Peter and the friars exemplified. During the discussion, Teresa's young niece Maria asked, "Why not become Discalced nuns ourselves?" It would prove to be the inspiration that drove Teresa to change the history of the Carmelites. The existing rule of Carmel, which allowed contemplative nuns to keep their worldly possessions and socialize in private apartments, no longer satisfied these women's spiritual longings. They were ready to live the reformed life of Discalced rule.

The relaxed rule of Carmel was due in part to the system of convent life widespread in those days. Monastic houses in Avila and elsewhere had been established mainly to serve the needs of the families of powerful aristocrats. By providing endowments for these religious houses, the wealthy bought a kind of security insurance for unmarried daughters, perpetual honor for their dynastic legacy, burial at designated chapels, and unending prayers for their souls. But these endowments came with many strings attached.

Endowments were meant to provide a comfortable living for the nuns and enable them to devote their time to "the continual vocal recitation of prayer in choir."[25] That sounds laudable, until one reads the small print describing what some patrons demanded in exchange for their endowments.

The demands of one particular patron, Bernardo Robles,

are described by historian Jodi Bilinkoff. Robles left a sizable endowment to Incarnation Convent in his will of 1513. In exchange for his gift, "Robles specified in minute detail how and where he was to be buried, and required that one nun continually kneel before the Blessed Sacrament, holding a candle in her hand, and pray for his soul." The nuns were to continue this practice twenty-four hours a day, seven days a week. The prayers had to be vocal prayers so that when benefactors dropped in for Mass they could see and hear for themselves whether the nuns were fulfilling their obligation.[26] It seems that the patrons wanted to make sure they were getting their money's worth.

In 1533, twenty years after his death, the nuns asked the pope for relief from this burdensome obligation, which the pope granted. But Robles' heirs threatened to withhold payments from the estate to the convent, and the nuns had to resume the day and night vigils for Robles and his descendants. For years the convent and benefactors argued over the endowment and its obligations. It was not until 1574 that the nuns finally were free from the terms of the original bequest.[27]

A New Command

Though discussions about reform were escalating, Teresa never saw herself as a reformer, even though she had been contemplating a more strict observance of the Carmelite rule for some time. In sixteenth-century Avila, institutions were reformed by the men. *Mujercilla*, "ignorant little women," were supposed to pray and reform only themselves. Moreover, Teresa thought she had enough to do working on herself, and she was comfortable at Incarnation Convent.

But the idea of founding a new convent continued to intrigue her.[28] So Teresa prayed for God's guidance on the matter. Her description of God's response is a marvelous expression of her determination and increasing self-confidence. She wrote that one day after Communion she received a command from the Lord to pursue her goal to found a convent named for St. Joseph, who "would keep watch over us at one door, and our Lady at the other, that Christ would remain with us, and that it would be a star shining with great splendor.... He said that I should tell my confessor what he commanded, that he was asking him not to go against this or hinder me from doing it."[29]

Teresa needed every bit of encouragement she received from God because her confessor apparently had not received the same message. When she presented the idea to Father Alvarez, he told her there was no way her plan could be put into practice. He foresaw extreme opposition from the city.

As an important regional and religious center in Spain, Avila was politically ruled by an entrenched aristocracy who exerted control over both secular and religious life. As part of her plan for reform, Teresa wanted independence from aristocratic control—especially from the endowments—to ensure that her new convent would not be tied to the demands of the wealthy. She instinctively knew that by insisting on poverty she could secure freedom from the demands of wealthy benefactors. She also foresaw how important this autonomy would be for the women in her convent who wanted the freedom to practice mental prayer.

But the antagonism and hostility she would soon face showed that the nobility and ecclesiastical authorities were not ready to give up control without a fight.[30]

Chapter 8
A CHALLENGE TO THE STATUS QUO

Father Baltasar Alvarez must have realized that Teresa was determined to establish a reformed Carmelite convent. Fortunately, he did not forbid her to follow her vision nor declare the command she had received was false. Instead, he suggested that she present her idea to the provincial of the Carmelites. Teresa, however, was disappointed with Alvarez's response. She had expected his enthusiastic support for the plans she believed God wanted her to carry out.

In a shrewd political move, Teresa decided to get the endorsement of other influential persons before she presented her plan to the provincial. One individual who gave her cause a big boost was Friar Peter of Alcantara, founder of the Discalced Franciscans and reputed to be a saintly ascetic. Teresa admired Peter for his holiness and found him "a delight to talk to, for he possessed a quick intelligence and subtle powers of discernment." Peter proved to be a kindred spirit who reassured Teresa about her mystical experiences, and he remained a friend and strong supporter of her reform until his death.[1]

Peter gave Teresa sound, practical advice for negotiating

her way through the formalities of gaining official approval. He had experienced the process himself when he had reformed the Franciscans, and he shared valuable suggestions for disarming opponents and gaining supporters, as well as tactics for getting papal approval and solving other logistical problems, such as securing a site and housing. One crucial supporter whom Peter himself had recruited was the Bishop of Avila, who would eventually approve Teresa's plan.

Teresa used her power of persuasion to enlist the help of others to her cause. When Father Pedro Ibanez and the influential Dominicans gave their endorsement, Teresa was ready to present her idea to the Carmelite provincial. Influenced by Teresa's reputation and that of her esteemed supporters, Provincial Angel de Salazar gave his permission for her first convent. But his consent would prove to be short-lived.

Trouble was brewing for Teresa on the home front. Some of the nuns at Incarnation Convent were circulating rumors and gossip against Teresa because they felt her reform plans were an insult to them. Did she consider herself better than they were? Some thought she should be sent to the convent prison for her arrogance. Even her confessor, Alvarez, scolded her for all the scandal she was causing and told her to "drop the matter once and for all."[2]

Understandably, Teresa's doubts returned. She wondered

if she were deceiving herself. Were her voices and visions nothing but dangerous illusions? Teresa turned to her supporter Father Ibanez for reassurance. She prepared an "Account of Conscience," a spiritual testimony that Ibanez subsequently endorsed for his fellow theologians. His approval helped Teresa through her personal crisis and strengthened her courage.[3]

Outcry in Avila

When word of Teresa's proposed convent got around Avila, uproar arose. "Who was Doña Teresa de Ahumada anyway to think that she could establish some new-fangled way of life? Avila did not need another convent. Who would provide for the nuns' upkeep?"[4] Fearful of the public outcry, Provincial de Salazar withdrew his permission for the convent. It looked as if the whole idea was dead and that Teresa's movement would be derailed by the negative reaction.

Why such fierce opposition to a few harmless nuns moving into a new convent? The reason given by city leaders was that a convent founded in poverty would be a drain on the local economy. However, another reason seems more likely to have contributed to the hostile response from the mayor and city council. Historian Jodi Bilinkoff reports that Avila's elites "possessed a vested interest in perpetuating the socio-religious system that Teresa of Jesus had come to reject."[5] By refusing a fixed income for the reformed Carmelite convents, Teresa's actions would break the control of the wealthy, who wanted to retain the convents as places where their daughters would be taken care of in a manner befitting upper-class status. And they wanted their family dynasty to be remembered on the convent walls long after they were gone.

A second reason for the opposition focused on Teresa's plan to encourage her nuns to practice mental prayer. This kind of private prayer was seen as an attempt to have a relationship with God that bypassed the ecclesiastical hierarchy. It was also considered a threat to the authority of the Church, which was a unifying force in Spanish society. In mid-sixteenth century, Spain felt threatened by the challenges to Church orthodoxy from the growing Protestant movement in other parts of Europe. Spain had become suspicious of any religious innovation that was not considered orthodox. Under Philip II, the fear of the threat of Protestant infiltration reached its height. Any whiff of rebellion was suspect, and the Inquisition was keen on picking up the scent. Spain turned dramatically repressive at the time Teresa was founding her reformed convents.

With her ideas about private, contemplative prayer, Teresa was treading on dangerous ground—especially since women were considered particularly susceptible to heretical ideas. Spain predictably reacted with panic at this "heresy" in the bastion of Catholicism, and the Inquisition intensified its repressive measures. Officials held firm to their stance that "any encouragement to personal and silent prayer was dangerous; all contact with God in this life must be indirect, mediated by the public means of historical revelation as set out by ecclesiastical authority."[6]

Yet Teresa was not about to give up her plan to found a new Carmel convent. After the Carmelite provincial withdrew his approval, she stayed silent for about five or six months—a long time for Teresa. But she wrote that she could not get out of her mind "that the foundation would be accomplished."[7]

Behind the Scenes

In April 1561, Teresa received good news. A new rector, Gaspar de Salazar, had been appointed to the Jesuit College of San Gil. When Teresa presented him with the reasons and arguments for her planned convent, he gave his whole-hearted support. This caused her confessor, Alvarez, who was vice-rector at the time, to change his mind. He lifted his ban on her plans and "even exhorted her to resume activity."[8] Freed from Alvarez's restraining order, Teresa continued full-speed ahead.

Unbeknownst to the authorities, when the Carmelite provincial had first refused to sanction Teresa's plan, she had decided to proceed "in all secrecy." Her plan was to present the provincial with a *fait accompli*.[9] She had slyly arranged to have her sister Juana purchase and furnish a house for the new convent, pretending it was for a married couple. Though penniless, Teresa had hired workmen to make adjustments to the building so it would be suitable for the nuns, and her brother Lorenzo had sent money to pay the workers. As work progressed, Teresa had worried that the provincial would find out what she was doing and put a stop to the whole project.

In July 1561, Teresa received another official blessing. Through her representative Doña Guiomar de Ulloa, she had secretly applied to Rome for a papal document to authorize the new Carmelite convent. The Bishop of Avila had approved the plan, placing it under his jurisdiction rather than under the jurisdiction of the Carmelite fathers. In other words, Teresa had circumvented the Carmelite provincial.

On the historic day of August 24, 1562, St. Joseph's Convent officially opened, with "the statues of Our Lady and St. Joseph set up over the doors and a small cracked bell hung in the belfry."[10]

Shortly after this joyful opening ceremony, Teresa wrote that she "found herself plagued by doubts of the severest kind." She suffered the tension between obeying official Church authority and following her own spiritual vision. Had she been disobedient by proceeding with her plans without the provincial's permission? Was it a good idea to place her convent under the rule of the bishop rather than the Carmelite order? Would she really be able to live the more austere life of absolute poverty in her new convent?[11]

During a period of prayer and reflection, Teresa remembered God's promises to her and renewed her commitment, determined to remain firm in following her vocation no matter what happened. Her doubts finally left her and she experienced great happiness.

But as she became more sure of herself, the civic authorities and citizens of Avila expressed their doubts more and more vocally in a citywide uproar.

Deadlock

The month the convent opened, the Avila town council held an emergency session to hear all those who objected to it. Their intention was to shut down St. Joseph's. As Teresa prepared to battle for her new convent, she received an order from the Prioress at Incarnation Convent to return at once and give an account of her actions. Since Teresa was still a member there, she was officially obligated to obey her superior. But before she left, Teresa wisely placed her four nuns at St. Joseph's under the care of the bishop.

It seems likely that city officials, fearful of Teresa's influence, conspired to remove her from her new convent. The town council quickly took advantage of her absence by trying to frighten the nuns into surrendering. The *Corregidor*, the king's representative, demanded that the nuns leave or he would order the doors battered down and have the nuns removed by force. The nuns fought back, saying they were not under his authority but the bishop's. They told him he should think twice about what he planned to do. A crowd gathered as the battle lines were drawn, with some people shouting abuse and others just curious.

The four courageous nuns prevented a break-in by reinforcing the doors with wooden beams. They had achieved a temporary victory. A brother of one of the nuns observed that "the commotion could not have been greater if the whole town were on fire or under attack by the Moors!"[12]

There was little Teresa could do to help her sisters; she could only watch from a distance at Incarnation Convent, and she had problems of her own to attend. She fully expected to be sent to the convent prison for her bold actions of reform. Instead of being dismayed at the idea, she thought perhaps prison would give her some needed peace and quiet after all the commotion.

But that did not happen. When the prioress, the community, and the provincial asked Teresa to give an account of her actions, she did so with eloquence, "explaining herself modestly and humbly, simulating more contrition than she felt" so they would know she was taking their objections seriously.[13] How could they think that she was offending the Order when all she wanted to do was to "serve its rule and traditions more perfectly?" She explained that she was not trying to draw attention to herself, and she freely admitted that she was more "wicked" than many of the other nuns.

Moved by her presentation, the listeners found no reason to condemn Teresa, and the provincial promised to let her return to St. Joseph's as soon as the uproar died down.[14] But the turmoil was not about to calm down any time soon.

When the town council realized that the nuns could not be intimidated into leaving, they referred the case to the Royal Council in Madrid. Frustrated, Teresa wrote, "I was amazed at all the efforts the Devil was making against a few poor women and how convinced everyone was that a dozen sisters and their prioress would bring great harm to the town."[15]

Meanwhile, Teresa's many supporters were working energetically to change public opinion in her favor. The town council met once again to debate whether to allow a religious house dependent on alms. This time, a young Dominican, who knew Teresa only by hearsay, presented an eloquent defense of her reform. Domingo Banez first asked the council members what big disaster they were expecting: foreign enemies, raging fire, pestilence, famine or other ruin? Why were they then so afraid of four barefooted nuns—poor, peaceful, virtuous? He argued: "Give me leave to say that to convoke so solemn a meeting for so slight a cause seems to me a lessening of the authority of so grave a city."[16]

Banez's powerful oratory made enough of an impression on the council members that they gave permission for the convent to stay open while the case was being decided in Madrid. As matters dragged on, Teresa's friends kept her informed of events, since she was still under orders to remain at Incarnation Convent. Finally, in November an official from the Royal Council arrived in Avila to take statements from the battling parties.

During the proceedings, Avila's councilors began to realize that the lawsuit was expensive and time-consuming and that they would have to compromise. So they offered Teresa a proposal saying they would tolerate the convent—*if* it would be adequately endowed.[17] With typical audacity, they drew up a compromise and simply expected Teresa to sign.

A New Beginning

Wearied by the battles and concerned for her embattled friends, Teresa began to have second thoughts about her stance on endowments. Should she show her willingness to compromise and accept a fixed endowment for St. Joseph's? If she agreed, she would put a stop to the endless fighting, and she reasoned that she could always change her policy regarding endowments later. Feeling at an impasse, Teresa prayed over the matter. She later wrote that the Lord told her "not to do any such thing, for once we agreed to live on the income from endowments, they would never let us do otherwise."[18] Given the checkered tradition of endowed convents, this proved to be astute political advice from the Lord.

As if to second the command, Teresa received a message in a vision from deceased Franciscan Peter of Alcantara, in which he repeated his earlier warning not to accept endowments. He pointedly asked why she was not following his advice. Jolted from a compromise position, Teresa made her decision: "Never would St. Joseph's accept a fixed endowment."[19]

Although many years later Teresa would relax her strict rule and accept limited financial help, at the time her goals were clear: She required her convents to be free from endowments and the burden of pleasing benefactors. She remembered the endless quarrels over benefactors' demands during her years at Incarnation Convent and wanted to ensure that—contrary to past practice—no one would be turned away from the new convent because she did not have a sizable dowry. Teresa also wanted all novices to be treated as equals, regardless of their social class.

In the end, Teresa refused to sign the proposed agreement, and the controversy dragged on. Teresa sent another petition to Rome, asking that the new convent be allowed to exist without the fixed financing provided by benefactors. While her opponents were struggling to find a solution, Teresa got a lucky break. The Dominican Pedro Ibanez, who had previously opposed the idea of a convent operating without a source of funding, changed his mind and gave his approval for the convent. He also encouraged the Carmelite provincial to allow Teresa to return to St. Joseph's.

Around March 1563, seven months after St. Joseph's Convent officially opened, Teresa was finally given permission to leave Incarnation Convent and moved to her new convent. "Leaving behind her shoes and her family pride" as well as her surname, she became Teresa of Jesus.[20] Teresa wrote that she experienced ecstatic joy when she entered the house of St. Joseph's: "I saw Christ, who seemed to be receiving me with great love and placing a crown on my head and thanking me for what I did for His Mother."[21]

The Papal Brief that would grant official permission for the convent to exist on public charity was not issued for another two years, on July 17, 1565, but in the ensuing months, public opposition turned around. The lawsuit was abandoned, and Teresa and her nuns were free to live the reformed life of Carmel in peace.

For four years, Teresa enjoyed the seclusion at St. Joseph's, which gave her time to write her *Way of Perfection* about her vision of the Carmelite vocation. It would be the last time, however, that Teresa would get a long period of rest and reflection. In 1567 this spirited Spanish woman embarked on a journey to establish sixteen more convents.

And the battles continued.

Chapter 9
A Bold Approach

After four peaceful years spent developing her Carmelite community of St. Joseph's, Teresa was eager to expand the reform beyond Avila. In 1567 her missionary zeal got a boost from a visiting Franciscan friar, Alonso Maldonado. He had just returned from the Indies and preached about all the lost souls who were neither baptized nor instructed in the Christian faith. Remembering her own horrid vision of hell, Teresa was determined to do something to prevent others from suffering such torment. She believed that a Carmelite community dedicated to a life of prayer "would take the place of Moses on the mountain, who ensured Israel's triumph over its enemies by keeping his hands raised in supplication while the battle raged in the plain beneath."[1]

Six months later, Teresa got her opportunity. In her *Book of Foundations*, she described the course of events. When the Carmelite Superior General, John Baptist Rossi (Rubeo), made a visit to St. Joseph's, Teresa was apprehensive that he might raise objections over the irregular way St. Joseph's had been placed under the jurisdiction of the bishop rather than the provincial of the order. Rather than remain silent, Teresa decided on a bold approach and told him the whole story of what had happened.

Rubeo was pleasantly surprised to discover all that Teresa had accomplished, and he realized it could have new meaning for him. Her reform embodied the goals of the recent Council of Trent, such as a return to the stricter form of religious life, which Rubeo was authorized to implement. Overjoyed at his response, Teresa told him of her plans for expanding the number of Discalced convents. Rubeo not only gave his approval for the expansion but also told her she could found "as many as the hairs on her head"—as long as they were to be limited to the province of Castile.[2]

A short time later, Teresa boldly asked permission to found Discalced Friaries for men—an unheard of request by a woman living in Catholic Spain in the sixteenth century. But for the time being, Teresa had her hands full fighting battles as she prepared to inaugurate her first reform convent outside of Avila, that of Medina del Campo.

Medina was a vibrant commercial center not far from Avila, and Teresa thought it a good choice for her second convent for several reasons. First, she expected there would be women of Medina who would welcome the reformed Carmelite life, especially women of *converso* background, converts from Judaism who were restricted from entering other convents. Teresa also had influential friends in Medina who supported her reform and could be counted on to enlist the support of other citizens. One friend, Fray Antonio de Heredia, even offered to secure housing for the convent. After the long battle to establish St. Joseph's, Teresa was determined to succeed more quickly in her next venture.

In August of 1567, Teresa and a small group of sisters—including two of her cousins—set off across the hot, rugged Castilian plain for Medina. Their chaplain, Julian de Avila, accompanied them on horseback, while the sisters traveled in a covered donkey cart driven by muleteers. It proved to be a difficult journey that took two days under the hot August sun. Fortified by the anticipation of moving into their new home and meeting friends who awaited their arrival, however, the delegation pressed on.

A Warning and a Welcome

When they reached Arevalo, halfway to Medina, Teresa received some bad news: The Augustinian Friars in Medina were opposed to her coming. They thought her temporary convent would be too close to their own house and did not want any competition for donations from the faithful. Because of their objections, the property owner had changed his mind and was now refusing to rent his house to the nuns. The friars sent a warning to Teresa to go back to Avila.

But Teresa and her party had traveled a long way under difficult conditions and were not about to return home. Besides, Teresa knew that if they went back they would be made the "laughing-stock of Avila" by those who thought the whole idea was crazy in the first place.[3]

Depressed, Teresa prayed for guidance and then moved into action. In order to spare her recruits the bad news, she sent all but two of them to stay with a relative until suitable housing could be found in Medina. She then dispatched Chaplain Julian on to Medina to make preparations for her arrival.

In the meantime, Teresa got good news that her friend Antonio had found another house that could be purchased for next to nothing—though she would later discover it was a tumbledown shack with holes in the roof, unfit for human habitation. She also learned that the Bishop of Avila was in Medina, and with clever foresight she arranged to meet with him to gain his support, which would be especially valuable in the event they faced hostility from the townspeople in Medina. After collecting supplies needed for their chapel, the group continued on to Medina.

They arrived shortly after midnight—a scheduling detail

that would become a regular part of Teresa's strategy for establishing future convents. By arriving in the middle of the night, she reasoned, they could move in and get everything ready for morning Mass before townspeople had an opportunity to object.

At the Carmelite monastery, they met Chaplain Julian and Teresa's friend Antonio, who helped them unload their cart. After gathering vestments and vessels for Mass, they made their way through the streets by torchlight toward the dilapidated house. Julian remarked that "they looked like a band of gypsies who had been robbing a church." If a watchman had spotted them, they would all have been thrown in prison.[4] Adding to the danger was the possibility of encountering one of the bulls that was being readied for the next day's bullfight.

Their relief in arriving at the house in Medina was short-lived. The condition of the house shocked Teresa, and she remarked that Antonio must be blind to have even considered such a place.[5] Working all night, they cleaned and repaired, adding religious wall hangings in a small porch section of the house that would be used for their first Mass in the morning.

Being a stickler for legality, Teresa knew it was crucial that the site be ready for an early first Mass. Once Mass had been said, the chapel would be officially "entered into service, it could not easily be dismantled or the religious house attached to it dissolved."[6]

Not one to let obstacles stop her, Teresa woke people in the middle of the night to get a sworn affidavit stating that the new convent had been founded with official approval.[7] This was another hard-earned lesson. Her experience in Avila had taught her that securing legal documents was crucial to heading off opposition.

The next morning with the celebration of Mass, the newest convent of St. Joseph was officially born. But Teresa's joy was tempered by the condition of the building that was expected to house the convent. In daylight it became clear that the house, with its crumbling walls and holes in the roof, was not suitable for habitation. In fact, the place was so flimsy that Teresa arranged for armed men to stand guard against intruders.

After a week of living in these deplorable conditions, the nuns received some relief. A local merchant offered the sisters a floor of his own home while they waited for repairmen to fix up the new convent. Two months later they moved back in, cheered by friends and eager new recruits.

The news of the success of the Medina convent opened new opportunities for Teresa. During the next four years, she founded seven more convents in the region of Castile. Each one presented a new set of problems: "city permissions to be sought, churchmen to pacify, quarrels to circumvent."[8] No matter the obstacle, however, Teresa was determined to overcome it.

And she almost always did.

Full Speed Ahead

One near-insurmountable obstacle arose in Toledo, the city where Teresa's grandfather had been humiliated by the Inquisition authorities nearly a century before. In order to establish a convent in Toledo, Teresa needed permission from Archbishop Bartolome de Carranza. But the archbishop had been imprisoned by the Inquisition for advocating mental prayer, and the vicar-general taking his place refused to issue a license. Undaunted, Teresa requested—and got—a personal interview with the vicar-general. In her *Book of Foundations* she wrote:

> When I saw him I told him that it was hard that there should be women anxious to live in such austerity and perfection, and strictly enclosed, while those who had never done any such thing themselves but were living a comfortable life should try to hinder work which was of such service to the Lord. I told him all this and a good deal more, speaking with a resoluteness with which I was inspired by the Lord. This touched his heart, and before I left he gave me the license.[9]

Armed with the license, Teresa set about full speed ahead to establish a house and present the citizens of Toledo with another of her *faits accompli*. As could be expected, members of the city council were angry when they discovered that "a mere woman had dared to make a foundation under their noses without their consent."[10] She was told to stop all activities immediately.

Teresa smoothed ruffled feathers and gained time to prepare her defense by telling council members she would do as they wished, even though she had been granted permission. In the meantime, she arranged to get a notarized confirmation of the vicar-general's consent. Faced with legal documentation, the council was forced to back down.[11]

The years between 1568 and 1571 found Teresa constantly on the move. Not only did she establish seven more convents and two monastic houses for friars, but she had to tactfully and patiently introduce the new recruits to the Discalced form of religious life. Adjusting to radical poverty and a more austere form of living was not easy.

The monastic houses proved to be particularly difficult for Teresa because of her inexperience working with male religious. Help with the male recruits turned up in the form of a five-foot tall, fervent friar who would come to be known as John of the Cross. Reputed to be saintly, John had a brilliant mind to match his religious zeal. Teresa had great admiration and respect for him, and he traveled with her to get first-hand experience of the Discalced rule as lived by the women religious.

Then in 1568, with John's help, Teresa inaugurated the first Discalced Carmelite reform adapted for men. The Duruelo Priory (thirty miles from Avila) opened with just two male recruits, Friar John of the Cross and Friar Antonio. But after an initial trial and error period of living the new reformed rule, the Duruelo Priory found itself faced with a steady stream of recruits who presented themselves for admission.

Teresa's reform ideal had successfully expanded to include male branches. But as the Discalced reform grew, opposition from the more relaxed branch increased, which led to fierce battles within the Carmelite community. Ultimately, this would impact Teresa's life in a very direct way.

Chapter 10
AN UNWELCOME SUMMONS

In 1571, while in the midst of solving some problems at her Medina convent, Teresa received a directive that stopped her in her tracks. She was ordered to become the Prioress at Incarnation Convent in Avila—a place she had deliberately left nine years earlier.

Needless to say, Teresa was not pleased. She would be sidelined again, taken away from her own convents "as they struggled to stabilize themselves in their respective cities."[1] The pretext given for the order was that Incarnation Convent badly needed reform. In June, a papal representative, Father Pedro Fernandez, had been visiting Avila on his mission to inspect religious houses. The local provincial, Angel de Salazar, who disliked the Discalced reforms, convinced Fernandez that Incarnation Convent needed someone to better manage its funds and to discourage frequent visitors—and that the best person for the job was Teresa. It is reasonable to suspect that his real motive for getting Teresa back was to slow her reforms and cause her own convents to wither away from lack of attention.

At the time, conflict raged between the reformed and unreformed branches of the Carmelite order. As the Discalced grew and became a challenge to the Calced, rivalry developed over the question of which interpretation of the Carmelite Rule was the authentic one. Each side was struggling for supremacy, and Teresa had become a lightning rod for the conflict. What better way to stop the spread of her work than to assign her a position that would demand all her time and attention?

Teresa must have been deeply torn between the need to shore up her own newly-created convents and the need to obey her superiors. Yet on July 10, 1571, she obediently accepted a three-year appointment as Prioress of Incarnation Convent. With a clear grasp of the battle she was about to face, Teresa took action to increase the chances of success. She knew that Incarnation Convent had become a social gathering place, attracting all manner of persons who had no intention of following a religious vocation. These people had become a drain on the meager resources of the convent. Before she moved in, therefore, Teresa insisted that all hangers-on be removed from the convent.

When she arrived at Incarnation Convent, Teresa quickly found that she was not wanted by many of the nuns, who considered her appointment interference and called her "a willing stooge." Teresa faced a hostile community who protested she would impose on them a way of life they had not chosen.[2] The battle lines were drawn: Provincial Salazar was determined she should move in; the nuns and their supporters were just as determined to keep her out.

A Police Escort

Teresa's move to Incarnation Convent must have been quite a scene. The provincial, anticipating trouble, arranged for her to be escorted by an agent of the Crown, several officers of the law, two Carmelite friars, and himself. As the procession moved toward the convent, it attracted a crowd of onlookers expecting a fight. Pandemonium broke out as they reached the convent door. Angry nuns blocked the entrance with their bodies, while "others shrieked and shook their fists defiantly, one fainted in the crush."[3]

In the midst of the chaos, a handful of Teresa's loyal supporters courageously welcomed her as they began singing the hymn *Te Deum*. The escort finally made its way through the barricade, and Teresa calmly walked inside. The convent door closed, and the escort party departed with a sigh of relief, thankful that no one had been injured. Once inside the solemn chapel, Teresa spoke in a quiet, gentle manner to calm everyone down. Then she went to her cell to prepare for her inauguration ceremony the next day.

With an amazing combination of divine inspiration and well-honed political skill, Teresa began her assignment with an act that diffused both opposition and hostility. When the nuns gathered to witness the inauguration of their new superior, they were stunned to discover that Teresa was not in the prioress' stall. Instead, a statue of Our Lady of Clemency holding the keys of the convent stood mutely waiting their arrival. "At her feet on the floor sat the prioress, her feet tucked neatly under her habit as was the custom among the Discalced. The symbolism was obvious—the Virgin, not Teresa, was to be the real guide of the community."[4]

In her address to the community, Teresa told the nuns that with the Lord's help she would serve them and learn from them as well. She reminded them that she herself was a daughter of Incarnation and reassured them that she would not impose her reformed way of life on them but would govern according to the rules they were accustomed to.

Teresa's respect for the individual human dignity of the nuns won over even the most rebellious. A month later Teresa wrote, "There is peace here now."[5] To ensure that the nuns had good spiritual guidance, Teresa brought in John of the Cross to be their confessor. John had exceptional gifts of insight and compassion. With his help, conditions at the convent rapidly improved.

"No" Is Not an Answer

By late 1574, Teresa began to turn her attention back to her own Discalced convents, which had been left floundering for nearly three years and desperately needed her guidance. Teresa was ready to go, but her superiors refused to release her because the Council of Trent had ruled that nuns should remain confined to their convents.

True to character, Teresa would not take "no" for an answer when she felt there was a pressing need. She sent a message via emissary to King Phillip II explaining her need to visit her reform convents. At the time, the Spanish monarchy and ecclesiastical authorities were at odds over who had control of Church reforms. Phillip supported the Discalced reform, so Teresa took advantage of the opportunity created by the conflict. The king agreed with Teresa's request and subsequently persuaded Pope Pius V to grant her permission to visit her convents.

In 1575, Teresa completed her term as Prioress of Incarnation Convent. She was nearly sixty years of age and suffered from many physical ailments, including a weak heart, frequent fevers, and arthritis that necessitated the use of a cane. But illness did not stop her. Teresa made travel plans not only to visit her existing convents but also to establish more.

Teresa's new convent at Beas de Segura in 1575 turned out

to be an occasion for joy as well as a cause of costly complications. At Beas, Teresa met Jerome Gratian, a young friar who would become her closest friend, confidant, and political ally until she died. Together they schemed and fought the fierce opposition from the Calced Carmelites who wanted to destroy the reform movement.

While at Beas, an unfortunate mistake on Teresa's part triggered a new set of problems. After the convent had been established, Teresa learned that contrary to what she had assumed Beas was not within the jurisdiction of Castile but rather was under the ecclesiastical authority of neighboring Andalusia. This put her in direct violation of the conditions under which Carmelite Superior General Rubeo had given approval for Teresa's expansion: that her convents be limited to Castile.

In the meanwhile, the governing body of the Calced Carmelites met in Rome and passed a resolution to suppress the Discalced. Teresa worried that the reform would die out. In July of 1575 she sent another urgent message to King Philip II. With her practical political sense, Teresa asked the king to make the Discalced into a separate province. The king supported Teresa's reform, but the pope's nephew supported the unreformed Carmelites and lined up forces to oppose Teresa. As in many arenas, the king and the pope rivaled one another for decision-making power. The impasse continued for many years until the Royal Council arranged a compromise to present to Rome. In 1580, after years of struggle, the Discalced Carmelites were finally granted autonomy by Pope Gregory XIII, and Gratian was elected the first provincial.

While the battle between the Calced and Discalced Carmelites raged, Teresa was sidelined by Superior General Rubeo. Angry because she had disobeyed his command to limit her convents to Castile, he ordered her to retire to a convent of her choice. Teresa later expressed sorrow that she was unable to clear up what she considered to be a misunderstanding between herself and Rubeo before he died.

Time to Write

Teresa chose to "retire" at her Toledo convent. While at Toledo, Provincial Gratian urged her to write a book on prayer and the spiritual life for her nuns, to replace her earlier autobiography, *Life*, which was then in the hands of the Inquisition. Despite physical illness and exhaustion, "the request of someone she loved as she loved Gratian mobilized Teresa to gather her strength and exert herself on the project, for love—human and divine—was the source of her creativity."[6] Teresa began work on *The Interior Castle* in June 1577.

Given the widespread suspicion and punishment by the

Inquisition of anyone other than "learned men" who dared to write about prayer, it must have been a difficult and risky undertaking. We can only marvel at the strategies Teresa employed to deflect the censors and ensure a receptive audience. Historian Alison Weber observes that Teresa craftily used a number of tactics in her writing to make it acceptable to the Inquisition's censors and the male hierarchy. One such tactic was her clever use of scripture passages. The Index of Prohibited Books, published in 1559, had ordered all vernacular translations of the Bible destroyed. The uneducated, especially women, were forbidden to have direct access to scripture. So when Teresa referred to a passage from scripture, she disguised her knowledge by pretending that she remembered something she had heard from an official source. She further camouflaged her authoritative use of scripture by such comments as, "I don't know if I'm remembering it correctly." Weber contends that had Teresa not used such "imprecision and approximation" her writing could easily have led to her being branded a heretic.[7]

By the time she had completed *The Interior Castle* in November of 1577, Teresa had created a classic in the literature of spirituality. *The Interior Castle* is written in conversational style, using the rich imagery of a castle to represent the soul and seven mansions within the castle to depict stages in the life of prayer. For nearly a decade after her death, some theologians continued to argue that her books should be banned. But by 1614, the date of her beatification, the Church had accepted her writings.

Shortly after finishing *The Interior Castle,* Teresa fell and broke her left arm. Set badly, it had to be rebroken and reset, which left her in constant pain. A young lay sister, Anne of Bartholomew, cared for the ailing Teresa and would remain her companion during her last years.

In 1579, a newly appointed vicar-general of Avila released Teresa from her enforced retirement and gave her permission to visit her convents and found new ones. Despite her physical limitations, Teresa took advantage of the freedom to inspect her convents and founded five new ones.

After Teresa founded her last convent in Burgos in 1582, she planned to return to her beloved St. Joseph's at Avila. Her health was rapidly deteriorating, and she likely wanted to spend her last days at home. But it was not to be.

Final Journey

Before Teresa had a chance to leave, she received an order from the Castile provincial to go to Alba de Tormes. The duchess of Alba had requested Teresa's presence to bless the approaching labor and delivery of her daughter-in-law.

Although Teresa was dying, she obeyed the order. Accompanied by Anne of Bartholomew, she started out on what would prove to be a dreadful, punishing trip. Perhaps because of the urgency of the summons, they did not have time to gather provisions, and Anne was unable to get food other than some withered figs for the ailing Teresa. As it turned out, when they reached Alba, they learned that the duchess' daughter-in-law had already given birth and Teresa was not needed after all. The two nuns rode on to the Carmelite community in Alba, where they were warmly welcomed and where Teresa would spend her last days.

Nine days later, Teresa suffered a severe hemorrhage from what is thought to have been uterine cancer. Near death, she spoke a few words to her sisters urging them to keep the Carmelite rule and constitution with "great perfection."[8] Teresa died peacefully in Anne's arms on October 4, 1582. According to legend, the room was bathed in a sweet fragrance that penetrated the entire convent.

Forty years later, in 1622, Pope Gregory XI canonized Teresa. On September 27, 1970, she became the first woman saint to be proclaimed Doctor of the Church by Pope Pius VI, followed a week later by St. Catherine of Siena. Teresa was named "Doctor of Prayer" by the pope.

In the last two decades of her life, Teresa had traveled an

incredible road. From angry authorities trying to break down the doors of her first reform convent in 1562, to the founding of seventeen convents and four monasteries, Teresa had overcome one obstacle after another. Motivated by missionary zeal, nourished by a deep spiritual life, and gifted with charm and political skill, Teresa of Avila had successfully challenged the status quo. Fending off secular and religious opposition, she had created her own model religious community. Ultimately, she changed the world for her followers, giving women and men today a lasting legacy of political courage and holiness.

Conclusion

Genevieve, Catherine and Teresa stepped into the public arena and responded to the critical needs of their times with courage and determination. Compassion for the suffering of others led them to pursue goals beyond those of their personal lives by getting involved in public life. Strong faith and personal conviction enabled them to overcome near-impossible odds that would have prevented less courageous individuals from taking action.

The obstacles to entering political life in the fifth, fourteenth and sixteenth centuries were enormous for these women. Cultural and religious restrictions prescribed narrow choices and limited movement for women. Before they could even think about entering the public arena, Genevieve, Catherine and Teresa had to overcome the culturally established mental and physical barriers that restricted women. In doing so, they suffered the censure of family and public opinion and often risked severe punishment and even death. But motivated by love of neighbor and deep spiritual faith, they left the safety of conventional roles and followed their calling. They plunged into the turmoil of politics and influenced public decisions and actions, keenly aware that political decisions have an impact for good or evil on people's lives.

It is important to remember that these women were not formally considered saints until after their deaths; during their lifetimes when they acted against conventional norms or challenged tradition they were more likely to be labeled disobedient, troublemakers, or even heretics. Each one had to find her own creative way to deal with institutional obstacles, since there was no obvious path to follow for women in those times in the Church.

Nor was there a blueprint for women showing them how to forge a public role in the arena of politics. Genevieve, Catherine and Teresa had no education in the complexities of public life, and traditional norms restricted their early involvement in activities outside the home that would have provided personal experience. Through trial and error, they gained political skill. Building on their natural leadership abilities, they wisely sought out learned and experienced individuals to advise and help them achieve their public goals. They challenged cultural restrictions of appropriate behavior for women and demonstrated uncommon courage and boldness as they forged public roles to influence political events.

Veneration of these holy women as saints came long after their courageous world struggles. Awareness of the political and cultural conditions of their times only adds to our admiration of their personal and spiritual lives. By seeing how they dealt with difficulties in public affairs, we can relate to them as realistic models for creative action in today's world. The stories of these holy heroines can inspire and fortify all of us—women and men—as we face the many challenges of the twenty-first century.

Notes

I. St. Genevieve of Paris, Fearless Leader
Chapter 1: Genevieve's Promise

1. Joël Schmidt, *Sainte Genevieve: Et la Fin de la Gaule Romaine*, 18-19.
2. Ibid., 14-16.
3. Ibid., 40.
4. Ibid., 26.
5. Quoted in Jo Ann McNamara and John E. Halborg, with E. Gordon Whatley, ed. and trans., *Sainted Women of the Dark Ages*, 20-21.
6. Ibid., 21.
7. Ibid., 21.
8. Ibid., 21-22.
9. Schmidt, *Sainte Genevieve*, 52-53.
10. Michel Rouche, *Clovis*, 483.
11. Schmidt, *Sainte Genevieve*, 72-79.
12. Ibid., 72-79.

Chapter 2: Attila's Threat

1. Marcel Brion, *Attila: The Scourge of God*, 87.
2. Robert Latouche, *Caesar to Charlemagne: The Beginnings of France*, 171.

3. Schmidt, *Sainte Genevieve*, 105-06.

4. Ibid., 104.

5. Ibid., 106.

6. Ibid., 106-07.

7. Ibid., 108.

8. Quoted in McNamara and Halborg, ed. and trans., *Sainted Women of the Dark Ages*, 23.

9. Richard Humble, *Warfare in the Middle Ages*, 32.

10. McNamara and Halborg, ed. and trans., *Sainted Women of the Dark Ages*, 24.

11. Schmidt, *Sainte Genevieve*, 123.

12. McNamara and Halborg, ed. and trans., *Sainted Women of the Dark Ages*, 27.

13. Gregory, Bishop of Tours, *History of the Franks*, xv.

14. Ibid., xix.

15. Ibid., xx.

16. Schmidt, *Sainte Genevieve*, 134.

17. Ibid., 146-49.

18. Ibid., 160.

Chapter 3: Genevieve's Triumph

1. Schmidt, *Sainte Genevieve*, 169-72.

2. Ibid., 169-72.

3. Ibid., 176.

4. McNamara and Halborg, ed. and trans., *Sainted Women of the Dark Ages*, 31.

5. Schmidt, *Sainte Genevieve*, 177.

6. Ibid., 177.

7. Ibid., 178.

8. McNamara and Halborg, ed. and trans., *Sainted Women of the Dark Ages*, 32.

9. Schmidt, *Sainte Genevieve*, 178-79.

10. Edward James, *The Franks*, 66.

11. Schmidt, *Sainte Genevieve*, 179.

12. Ibid., 180.

13. Ibid., 179.

14. James, *The Franks*, 84.

15. Schmidt, *Sainte Genevieve*, 181-82.

16. Maurice Druon, *The History of Paris: From Caesar to Saint Louis*, 28.

17. Ibid., 28.

18. McNamara and Halborg, ed., and trans., *Sainted Women of the Dark Ages*, 36.

19. Schmidt, *Sainte Genevieve*, 185-86.

20. Peter Brown, *Society and the Holy in Late Antiquity*, 7.

21. Peter Brown, *The Cult of the Saints: Its Rise and Function in Latin Christianity*, 3-4.

22. Schmidt, *Sainte Genevieve*, 186-87.

II. Catherine of Siena, Diplomat
Chapter 4: From Prayer Cell to Political Hell

1. Edmund G. Gardner, *Saint Catherine of Siena: A Study in the Religion, Literature, and History of the Fourteenth Century in Italy*, 239.

2. Quoted in Sigrid Undset, *Catherine of Siena*, 82.

3. Ibid., 213-14.

4. Ibid., 215.

5. Raymond of Capua, *The Life of Catherine of Siena*, 24.

6. Richard Kieckhefer, *Unquiet Souls: Fourteenth-Century Saints and Their Religious Milieu*, 200.

7. Ibid., 138.

8. Raymond of Capua, *The Life of Catherine of Siena*, 45.

9. Ibid., 114.

10. Ibid., 116-17.

11. Ibid., 124.

12. Gardner, *Saint Catherine of Siena*, 112.

13. Suzanne Noffke, *Catherine of Siena: Vision Through a Distant Eye*, 57.

14. Ibid., 84.

15. Barbara W. Tuchman, *A Distant Mirror: The Calamitous 14th Century*, 29.

16. Quoted in Johannes Jorgensen, *Saint Catherine of Siena*, 160.

17. Ibid., 218.

Chapter 5: A Confrontation with the Pope

1. Johannes Jorgensen, *Saint Catherine of Siena*, 229.
2. Ibid., 229.
3. Gardner, *Saint Catherine of Siena*, 182.
4. Ibid., 182-83.
5. Ibid., 183.
6. Jorgensen, *Saint Catherine of Siena*, 232.
7. Gardner, *Saint Catherine of Siena*, 187.
8. Ibid., 187.
9. Giuliana Cavallini, *Catherine of Siena*, 12.
10. Jorgensen, *Saint Catherine of Siena*, 237.
11. Ibid., 245.
12. Gardner, *Saint Catherine of Siena*, 196.
13. Ibid., 198-99.
14. Undset, *Catherine of Siena*, 195.

Chapter 6: Success in Florence, Failure in Rome

1. Gardner, *Saint Catherine of Siena*, 211.
2. Karen Scott, "St. Catherine of Siena, 'Apostola'" *Church History*, Issue 61, (1992): 39.
3. Quoted in Gardner, *Saint Catherine of Siena*, 213.
4. John Temple-Leader and Giuseppe Marcotti, *Sir John Hawkwood: Story of a Condottiere*, 118-21.
5. Jorgensen, *Saint Catherine of Siena*, 251-52.
6. Ibid., 280.

7. Ibid., 281.

8. Gardner, *Saint Catherine of Siena*, 235-36.

9. Ibid., 235.

10. Tuchman, *A Distant Mirror*, 330.

11. Jorgensen, *Saint Catherine of Siena*, 285.

12. Ibid., 289-90.

13. Ibid., 290.

14. Ibid., 290.

15. Tuchman, *A Distant Mirror*, 329-30.

16. Undset, *Catherine of Siena*, 225-26.

17. Joseph Berrigan, "The Tuscan Visionary: Saint Catherine of Siena" in *Medieval Women Writers*, 261-62.

18. Cavallini, *Catherine of Siena*, 19.

19. Jorgensen, *Saint Catherine of Siena*, 323.

20. Ibid., 324.

21. Gardner, *Saint Catherine of Siena*, 289.

22. Ibid., 290.

23. Cavallini, *Catherine of Siena*, 121.

24. Undset, *Catherine of Siena*, 267.

25. Jorgensen, *Saint Catherine of Siena*, 369.

26. Ibid., 372.

III. St. Teresa of Avila, Reformer
Chapter 7: Tainted Blood

1. Stephen Clissold, *St. Teresa of Avila*, 96.
2. Alison Weber, *Teresa of Avila and the Rhetoric of Femininity*, 8-9.
3. Clissold, *St. Teresa of Avila*, 5-6.
4. Ibid., 11-12.
5. Kieran Kavanaugh and Otilio Rodriguez, trans., *The Collected Works of St. Teresa of Avila, Vol. One*, 54.
6. E. Allison Peers, *Handbook to the Life and Times of St. Teresa and St. John of the Cross*, 67.
7. Kavanaugh and Rodriguez,, trans., *The Collected Works of St. Teresa of Avila, Vol. One*, 58.
8. Ibid., 61.
9. Elizabeth Ruth Obbard, *La Madre: The Life and Spirituality of Teresa of Avila*, 22.
10. Clissold, *St. Teresa of Avila*, 22.
11. Kavanaugh and Rodriguez, trans., *The Collected Works of St. Teresa of Avila, Vol. One*, 64.
12. Clissold, *St. Teresa of Avila*, 25-26.
13. Kavanaugh and Rodriguez, trans., *The Collected Works of St. Teresa of Avila, Vol. One*, 65.
14. Clissold, *St. Teresa of Avila*, 27-28.
15. Kavanaugh and Rodriguez, trans., *The Collected Works of St. Teresa of Avila, Vol. One*, 66-67.

16. Obbard, *La Madre*, 36-37.

17. Clissold, *St. Teresa of Avila*, 35.

18. Jodi Bilinkoff, *The Avila of Saint Teresa: Religious Reform in a Sixteenth-Century City*, xii.

19. Clissold, *St. Teresa of Avila*, 44.

20. Cathleen Medwick, *Teresa of Avila: The Progress of a Soul*, 40-42.

21. Ibid., 40-42.

22. Clissold, *St. Teresa of Avila*, 53.

23. Kavanaugh and Rodriguez, trans., *The Collected Works of St. Teresa of Avila, Vol. One*, 276-78.

24. Ibid, *Vol. Three*, 20.

25. Bilinkoff, *The Avila of Saint Teresa*, 35-38.

26. Ibid., 50-51.

27. Ibid., 50-51.

28. Obbard, *La Madre*, 54-55.

29. Kavanaugh and Rodriguez, trans., *The Collected Works of St. Teresa of Avila, Vol. One*, 280-81.

30. Weber, *Teresa of Avila and the Rhetoric of Femininity*, 124.

Chapter 8: A Challenge to the Status Quo

1. Clissold, *St. Teresa of Avila*, 73.

2. Ibid., 75.

3. Ibid., 76.

4. Obbard, *La Madre*, 58.

5. Bilinkoff, *The Avila of Saint Teresa*, 140.

6. Rowan Williams, *Teresa of Avila*, 28-30.

7. Kavanaugh and Rodriguez, trans., *The Collected Works of St. Teresa of Avila, Vol. One*, 288.

8. Clissold, *St. Teresa of Avila*, 79.

9. Peers, *Handbook to the Life and Times of St. Teresa and St. John of the Cross*, 8.

10. Obbard, *La Madre*, 62.

11. Ibid., 63.

12. Clissold, *St. Teresa of Avila*, 96-97.

13. Obbard, *La Madre*, 65.

14. Clissold, *St. Teresa of Avila*, 98.

15. Ibid., 99.

16. Obbard, *La Madre*, 66.

17. Clissold, *St. Teresa of Avila*, 99.

18. Ibid., 99.

19. Obbard, *La Madre*, 67.

20. Medwick, *Teresa of Avila*, 89.

21. Kavanaugh and Rodriguez, trans., *The Collected Works of St. Teresa of Avila, Vol. One*, 320.

Chapter 9: A Bold Approach

1. Obbard, *La Madre*, 79.

2. Medwick, *Teresa of Avila*, 117.

3. Clissold, *St. Teresa of Avila*, 130-31.

4. Medwick, *Teresa of Avila*, 120.

5. Obbard, *La Madre*, 86.

6. Clissold, *St. Teresa of Avila*, 132.

7. Ibid., 132.

8. Quoted in Obbard, *La Madre*, 93.

9. Ibid., 93-94.

10. Clissold, *St. Teresa of Avila*, 140.

11. Ibid., 140.

Chapter 10: An Unwelcome Summons

1. Obbard, *La Madre*, 100.

2. Clissold, *St. Teresa of Avila*, 153.

3. Obbard, *La Madre*, 102.

4. Ibid., 103.

5. Peers, *Handbook to the Life and Times of St. Teresa and St. John of the Cross*, 19.

6. Obbard, *La Madre*, 128.

7. Weber, *Teresa of Avila and the Rhetoric of Femininity*, 106.

8. Obbard, *La Madre*, 149.

Resource Guide

St. Genevieve of Paris

Brion, Marcel. *Attila: The Scourge of God.* Translated by Harold Ward. London: Cassell and Company, Ltd., 1929.

Brown, Peter. *The Cult of the Saints: Its Rise and Function in Latin Christianity.* Chicago: University of Chicago Press, 1981.

———. *Society and the Holy in Late Antiquity.* Berkeley, CA: University of California Press, 1982.

Contamine, Philippe. *War in the Middle Ages.* Translated by Michael Jones. Cambridge, MA: Blackwell Publishers Ltd., 1984.

Druon, Maurice. *The History of Paris: From Caesar to Saint Louis.* Translated by Humphrey Hare. London: Rupert Hart-Davis, 1969.

Gregory, Bishop of Tours. *History of the Franks.* Selections, translated with notes by Ernest Brehaut. New York: W.W. Norton & Company, Inc., 1969.

Humble, Richard. *Warfare in the Middle Ages.* New York: The Mallard Press, 1989.

James, Edward. *The Franks.* New York: Basil Blackwell Inc., 1988.

Latouche, Robert. *Caesar to Charlemagne: The Beginnings of France.* Translated by Jennifer Nicholson. New York: Barnes & Noble, Inc., 1968.

McNamara, Jo Ann, and John E. Halborg, with E. Gordon Whatley, eds. and trans. *Sainted Women of the Dark Ages.* Durham, NC: Duke University Press, 1992.

Rouche, Michel. *Clovis.* Paris: Fayard, 1996.

Schmidt, Joël. *Sainte Genevieve: Et la Fin de la Gaule Romaine.* Paris: Perrin, 1990. Used with written permission.

Wemple, Suzanne Fonay. *Women in Frankish Society: Marriage and the Cloister, 500 to 900.* Philadelphia: University of Pennsylvania Press, 1981.

St. Catherine of Siena

Berrigan, Joseph. "The Tuscan Visionary: Saint Catherine of Siena." *Medieval Women Writers.* Ed. Katharina M. Wilson. Athens, GA: University of Georgia Press, 1984.

Cavallini, Giuliana. *Catherine of Siena.* New York: Geoffrey Chapman, 1998.

Gardner, Edmund G. *Saint Catherine of Siena: A Study in the Religion, Literature and History of the Fourteenth Century in Italy.* New York: E. P. Dutton & Co., 1907.

Jorgensen, Johannes. *Saint Catherine of Siena.* Translated by Ingeborg Lund. New York: Longmans, Green and Co., 1938.

Kieckhefer, Richard. *Unquiet Souls: Fourteenth-Century Saints and Their Religious Milieu.* Chicago: University of Chicago Press: 1984.

McBrien, Richard P. *Lives of the Popes: The Pontiffs from St. Peter to John Paul II.* New York: HarperCollins, 1997.

Noffke, Suzanne. *Catherine of Siena: Vision Through a Distant Eye.* Collegeville, MN: The Liturgical Press, 1996.

Noffke, Suzanne, trans. *The Letters of Catherine of Siena.* Tempe, AZ: Arizona Center for Medieval and Renaissance Studies, 2000.

Raymond of Capua. *The Life of Catherine of Siena.* Translated, introduced and annotated by Conleth Kearns. Dublin: Dominican Publications, 1980.

Scott, Karen. "*St. Catherine of Siena, 'Apostola.' *" *Church History*, Issue 61, (1992): 34-46.

Temple-Leader, John, and Giuseppe Marcotti. *Sir John Hawkwood: Story of a Condottiere.* London: 1889.

Tuchman, Barbara W. *A Distant Mirror: The Calamitous 14th Century.* New York: Ballantine Books, 1978.

Undset, Sigrid. *Catherine of Siena.* Translated by Kate Austin-Lund. New York: Sheed and Ward, 1954.

St. Teresa of Avila

Bilinkoff, Jodi. *The Avila of Saint Teresa: Religious Reform in a Sixteenth-Century City.* Ithaca, NY: Cornell University Press, 1989. Quotations used with written permission.

Clissold, Stephen. *St. Teresa of Avila.* London: Sheldon Press, 1979.

Kavanaugh, Kieran, and Otilio Rodriguez, trans. *The Collected Works of St. Teresa of Avila*, 3 vols. Washington, DC:

Institute of Carmelite Studies, 1976-1985. Quotations used with written permission.

Medwick, Cathleen. *Teresa of Avila: The Progress of a Soul.* New York: Doubleday, 1999.

Obbard, Elizabeth Ruth. *La Madre: The Life and Spirituality of Teresa of Avila.* United Kingdom: St. Pauls, 1994.

Peers, E. Allison. *Handbook to the Life and Times of St. Teresa and St. John of the Cross.* London: Burns Oates, 1954.

Weber, Alison. *Teresa of Avila and the Rhetoric of Femininity.* Princeton, NJ: Princeton University Press, 1990.

Williams, Rowan. *Teresa of Avila.* Harrisburg, PA: Morehouse Publishing, 1991.

Acknowledgments

Many people deserve my gratitude for their generous assistance in making this book possible.

I especially want to thank my resourceful research assistant and French translator, Janine Free, who spent many hours translating French texts for the *Genevieve* section. She also helped locate difficult-to-find books in the United States and France.

Thanks to Latin translator Sr. Issac Jogues Rousseau, SSND, of Mount Mary College (Milwaukee, WI) for checking every detail of an English translation of Genevieve's *Vita Sanctae Genovefae* for accuracy. Many thanks to Sr. Mary Ann Sadowski, SSND, for locating a skillful Latin scholar.

I am grateful to History Professor Frank Stricker (California State University-Dominguez Hills) for his careful critique of the manuscript and for sharing his insights and expertise. This book benefits from his valuable advice to include the larger historical context of these stories.

Religious Studies Professor William Hagan (California State University-Dominguez Hills) read the manuscript with his experienced eye for historical accuracy and detail, and offered thoughtful suggestions for which I thank him.

Individuals who read early drafts and gave me valuable feedback include Mari Agnew, Terese Agnew, Sr. Laura J. Abat, OSF, and Sr. Michele McQueeney, OSF. Thank you!

Donna Kordela, writer and educator, offered valuable advice and writing tips. Many others who encouraged and sustained me during the years it took to write this book include Barb Agnew, Lou Agnew, Kathy Agnew and Irene DeGrasse. Thank you all!

I am grateful to the faculty of Alverno College (Milwaukee, WI) for providing the stimulus for scholarly excellence at a critical time in my life.

A big load of gratitude goes to computer gurus who rescued me from technical glitches numerous times: Fred Wiese, Sue Wahl, Olga Agnew and Sean Agnew.

It has been a privilege to work with Greg Pierce, president and co-publisher of ACTA Publications. I thank him for his faith in this book and for accepting it for publication. Thanks also to staff members at ACTA Publications for their dedication and work on this project. I wish to express special thanks to Nicole Kramer for her enthusiasm, support and initial critique of this book.

Editor Marcia Broucek has added wonderful narrative touches to this manuscript. Her meticulous attention to detail and her ear for fine-tuning the prose have made this a better book. I gratefully acknowledge her contribution.

I am thankful above all to my husband, Charlie Williams, for patiently reading early and late drafts of the manuscript and for offering his thoughtful criticisms and comments. He supported this project every step of the way and kept me going during difficult stages.

BOOKS ON PRAYER AND SPIRITUALITY

MIDWIVES OF AN UNNAMED FUTURE
Spirituality for Women in Times of Unprecedented Change
by MARY RUTH BROZ, RSM, and BARBARA FLYNN
with photographs by JEAN CLOUGH

A book for women who are passionate about exploring their role in shaping the "unnamed future," this unique series of reflections and rituals can be used by individuals or groups of women coming together to deepen their own spirituality and uncover new life in age-old spiritual truths. 208-page hardcover, $14.95

ALLEGORIES OF HEAVEN
An Artist Explores the "Greatest Story Ever Told"
by DINAH ROE KENDALL
with "The Message" text by EUGENE H. PETERSON

Contemporary English artist Dinah Roe Kendall offers a vibrant visual retelling of the full scope of Jesus' ministry through her figurative and narrative paintings, accompanied by Eugene Peterson's widely acclaimed contemporary rendering of the Bible. 100-page, four-color hardcover, $14.95

RUNNING INTO THE ARMS OF GOD
Stories of Prayer/Prayer as Story
by PATRICK HANNON

Stories of prayer in everyday life tied to the traditional hours of the monastic day: matins, lauds, prime, terce, sext, none, vespers, compline. 128-page hardcover, $15.95; paperback, $11.95

PRAYERS FROM AROUND THE WORLD
AND ACROSS THE AGES
compiled by VICTOR M. PARACHIN

A wealth of sublime, reverent and poignant prayers from many of the world's greatest spiritual practitioners, preceded by a one-paragraph biography of the person who composed it. 160-page paperback, $9.95

HENRI NOUWEN ILLUMINATED
by LEN SROKA

Significant and poignant words from spiritual master Henri Nouwen are brought to life in a new way, blended tastefully and delicately with contemporary photos. 160-page, four-color hardcover, $14.95